HOW TO LEA
& KEEP THE RIGHT BALANCE

The Leadership Matrix™

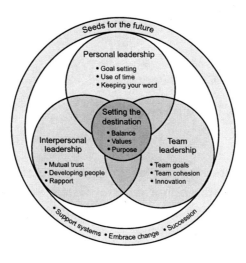

© 2007 Charles Barnascone

a story about Tom and The Magician
and a Leadership Workbook

CHARLES BARNASCONE

How to Lead Your Team... & Keep the Right Balance

Published by Wisdom Publishing Ltd

Tel 01636 629002

Copyright © Charles Barnascone 2007

Co-writer Christine Searancke

Editor: Ingrid St Clare

Editorial contributions: Laurice Barnascone, Tina Newton

Design: Charlotte Mouncey

ISBN: 978-0-9558787-1-8

This book is dedicated to my wife Laurice, who has been a constant source of love, learning and inspiration, to our four-year-old daughter Serena who challenges and entertains me with equal measure, and to my late father Peter who gave me all the love and support a son could wish for.

To Mamary
Thank you for the copy of
Appointments with Heaven
It was lovely to meet you and
I hope you found the Chat useful
Very best wishes

Contents

Tom and The Magician

Testimonials:

This is a great story, which is easily read, with the principles of leadership shining through very clearly.

The story isn't just about business, but how the principles of leadership affect and shape all parts of our lives.

A really enjoyable read, a must for all business leaders, and people seeking balance in their lives.

Chris Jones
Managing Director, t3 Retail Design Ltd.

What I have read is great and so easy to understand and follow. Once you start reading you are not able to stop - which I suppose for a book is the whole idea. Good luck.

Paul Lilicrap
General Manager, Newark Showground

I enjoyed the read - it contained what you had previously told/taught me at training courses, but in a more memorable and conceptual way.

A dry presentation of bullet points and diagrams are all very well - but a story really helps visualise pitfalls and how they manifest themselves in your work and personal life.

Martin Black
Director of Sales, Rexson Systems Limited

The philosophical Banascone approach is inspirational, early on I found myself wanting to read further and not put it down.

Leaders and managers from all walks of life can easily identify with Tom.

Light hearted straightforward reading reminding the reader of the many responsibilities of an effective leader.

The link between the text and reflections ensures that vital and practical learning does not get lost.

Fred Parsons
Director, NORSACA Adult & Further Education Services

A question of leadership provides valuable insights into all too familiar challenges faced by business leaders. It genuinely captures the power and simplicity of the key principles of leadership, asking fundamental questions and allowing the reader to complete tasks along their journey. We all need our own magician.

Ruth Appleton
Operations Director, Barker Ross Recruitment

I really enjoyed reading the book - although the concepts initially appear familiar, the way they are presented and more importantly linked is refreshing and memorable. The story of Tom and The Magician clearly demonstrates the day to day challenges that we all encounter in our personal and business lives, and goes on to provide a clear roadmap as to how we can break down these challenges into their constituent parts and then build up the answers back into an overall strategy for continuing success. The '5 circle' visualization of the Leadership Matrix then provides a clear, concise reminder of the behaviours necessary for success and deserves a place on every leaders wall.

P Howlett White BEng (Hons) CEng FIStructE
Managing Director, Terrapin Limited

Tom and the Magician is written in a style which is very easy to digest and allows the reader to see themselves in situations very similar to their own. The simple exercises can be applied to almost any work or family situations which enables you to work on getting the "Balance" right, probably the most important aspect of the book for me. A great quality of this book is that it does not make any comparisons or referrals to world renowned organisations or business leaders. It simply allows the reader to enjoy and maximize their own potential and personal success through others.

Des Duddy
Managing Director, Joinery Fit-Out Supplies

For the first time, a book that not only gives me the tools and techniques I need but also, helps me find the mental space to be able to use them fully and with best effect.

It is refreshing to read how important it is to achieve a good work/life balance. The concept is so simple and obvious and yet so easily overlooked. How can we be inspirational leaders without being inspired ourselves. How can we give a sense of purpose without having one ourselves and setting clear goals to achieve them. Only then can we lead by example.

Before I buy any book, I always read the first couple of pages to see if I could get 'into it'. As I read the first few chapters, I found I could so easily relate to Tom. In reading the story and then looking at the reflections, I could see how Tom's story related to me and what I could do to develop my leadership skills.

A very practical and useful insight into modern leadership thinking.

Steve Templeman
Regional Manager, Legal Services Commission

Stand out from the crowd by doing something lots of other people do and do it differently - and do it well. In 'Tom & The Magician' Charles and Christine have done just that, and take us on a journey many of us will recognise.

So much hit home and at the end I was left with a reminder of an Inescapable Truth: ' Only I Am The Expert On Me' - and the clues are all around me.

So in the end the only question which matters is this: 'How well are we paying attention?'

This book well and truly sets us on our way.

Andy Mouncey
Managing Director, Doing Big and Scary

Chapters one and two have whet my appetite for the whole book what I have read has motivated me to review the balance of the business and my leadership role.

Mark Read
Managing Director, ODB Group, Surrey

Acknowledgements

I owe a huge debt of gratitude to the many people who have helped with this book. One of the absolute joys of training people, is that I'm constantly learning at the same time. I often say that I learn from my delegates as they learn from me. So if you have attended my workshops, you have probably contributed to this book in some way. Thank you.

Many people have provided kind comments, and words of encouragement about the book, some of whom were prepared to allow me to place their comments in print and by inclusion they have been acknowledged personally. Thank you to everyone who has provided ideas and contributions.

Thank you to Richard Wilkins who kindly agreed to provide the foreward to this book. Richard you are a constant source of inspiration to me.

Thank you to the staff at Infinite Possibilities Ltd, both past and present, who have contributed to the success of our business, and created an environment where this book could be created.

A huge thank you to Laurice Barnascone, Tina Newton, and Ingrid St Clare, who worked patiently through the text, several times to make sure that I had communicated my messages clearly, and who provided invaluable feedback and support when it was necessary.

Thank you to Charlotte Mouncey, who brilliantly executed the design, and converted a whole heap of text and diagrams into something very readable, of which we can all be justifiably proud.

Finally, thank you to Christine Searancke, without whom this book would simply not have been possible. When my father died, my writing just stopped, and Christine gently picked up the pieces and breathed it all back to life. Thank you from the bottom of my heart, for the incredible contribution you have made to my life, my business, and this book.

Foreword by Richard Wilkins

Tom and The Magician is far more than a book, it's a wonderful opportunity to discover The Magician in you and as you'll discover, that will change everything!

I love the way we're guided to see how we can create true balance between the home and work, how we're drip fed so many valuable lessons through the wisdom of The Magician whilst we follow Tom through challenges and triumphs we can all relate to.

This is a book that people need to read, how can it not be when the phrase... *"So are you busy?"* ...Is still the most common way we attempt to ascertain if someone is successful. Busy-ness does not equal success, it uses up lives.

People are not struggling because they have too much quality time with their family. The strength of this little gem of a book is that it offers us a way to achieve 'success without busy-ness'.

The danger for all of us is that we become isolated, lost and lonely and look back on the relationship with our family with regret, but that doesn't need to be anymore, not once we discover our newfound companions, this book and The Magician within us.

As you turn through the pages it's as if the mist of confusion and complication lifts to reveal The Magician, so a huge thank you to Charles for allowing The Magician in you to awaken The Magician in us.

Richard Wilkins   www.theministryofinspiration.com

Getting the most from this book

How you read this book is up to you and will depend on your personal learning style and level of experience as a leader. You can read the story right through and then go on to the reflections on the concepts and the tasks, or you can read a chapter and then go to the reflections and tasks for that particular chapter.

The important thing is that you actually do the exercises. This is what will make all the difference to your behaviours as a leader. Getting familiar with concepts intellectually is one thing, but it is nothing like as powerful as getting to grips with them practically. You need to apply them to your real-life situations whether at home or work.

When you do the tasks, give yourself the time and space to do them properly rather than rushing. Also, realise that if you are going to make a real difference to the way you lead others, it will take time. Set yourself realistic targets and celebrate small successes as you progress. This way you will integrate the changes into everything that you do and improve your leadership in all aspects of life.

A word about pronouns. Throughout the book I have tried to balance gender. Within the story there is a mix of characters to reflect this. In the concepts section I have loosely alternated between my use of the male or female gender, simply because this is how the book flowed. The concepts of leadership are not gender specific, it is simply easier to read than continually having 'his or her', or 'him or her', when giving explanation. Overall it is the concept that is more important than which gender I refer to, and I hope this comes across when you read.

Finally, if you think that you recognise some of the characters, this is entirely coincidental. This is a fictional story with imaginary people, but they and the situations in which they find themselves are very much based on real life.

Chapter 1 – Time for change

Tom was glad the week was over. With Christmas coming up it was a short month anyway and he was looking forward to the end of a pretty tough year. The business needed to hit its targets with only a three-week month and his team seemed to be more focussed on Christmas festivities than on achieving targets. To make matters worse, payments due in at the end of this month had been delayed, clients were unwilling to give specific commitments, and he still had December's salaries to pay. All this was putting Tom under tremendous stress, at a time supposed to be about goodwill to all men.

"Bloomin' Christmas," muttered Tom as he headed home, the day before Christmas Eve. "I hope somebody releases some money tomorrow or we're going to be right in it."

To this day, Tom couldn't be sure why he drove via the coast that day. He didn't normally, and he needed to get home. But something inside him took him that way. Funny isn't it how your unconscious mind can take you to places you wouldn't normally go for answers you wouldn't normally get?

It was a beautiful evening, clear and cool but not too cold, with a slight breeze. Tom drove out of town through the outskirts of Bosmouth and onto the coast road. Eventually he stopped to look over the estuary and out to sea. He seemed to be able to think more clearly when he was near the sea. It must be something about the rhythm of the waves. Tom decided to go for a walk. "A quick walk in the fresh air," he thought, "I'll only be five minutes, and it'll clear my head." He parked the car, and headed off down the coastal path toward the boathouse of the Bosmouth Sailing Club. "Just as far as the clubhouse and back, that'll be far enough, then I need to get home to prepare for tomorrow."

Unsurprisingly for this time of year the area seemed deserted, just a few dog walkers. Tom sat on a bench, pausing to reflect for a while before heading back to his car.

"Lovely evening," said a voice in Tom's ear. Tom was startled. There to his right sat a man who seemed vaguely familiar.

"Yes, it is. I felt drawn to stop and walk by the sea," said Tom.

"Restoring balance?" pondered the man.

"How do you mean?" asked Tom.

"Well, everything craves balance," said the man, "it's nature's way. Look out to the ocean, there's always movement, it's always changing, yet there's always balance. Think of the seagulls, the way they wheel and turn, constantly responding to the world around them: the sea, the sky, the wind and the fish they want for dinner!"

Tom reflected, what the man said made sense. He knew it deep inside, but somehow he'd forgotten.

"I must admit things have been a bit stressful recently, and when I come to think about it, I tend to relax by getting away from it all and connecting with nature," said Tom.

"We all have our own way of regaining balance, it's essential for our well-being," said the man. "Do you see the lights on that yacht out there? Sailors know how to work with the elements; they are constantly adjusting to the tides, the currents, and the subtle changes in the wind's direction, always steering a steady course by continually balancing one force with another. When the wind changes, they may adjust the sails; when the current moves, they may raise the centreboard and when the clouds are ominous they might head for port."

Tom nodded; it struck a chord with him. He remembered how energised he'd felt when he started the business. Things hadn't always gone according to plan, but he'd discovered ways around it and made things happen. His old skills seemed to have left him, these days every tiny squall became a major challenge. He was irritable, fed up and frustrated and to top it all his back pain was playing him up. His wife had said only this morning that he'd been working too hard, and that if he wasn't careful he'd be getting a bad back again.

"It's not that easy to get balance though is it?" said Tom "I'd like greater balance in my life but somehow circumstances don't allow it at present, stress seems the norm, I try to stay positive but it doesn't always work."

"I'm not talking about being positive," said the man. "I'm talking about balance. Being positive all the time can make things worse not better. Balance is about embracing positive and negative and using them both. Think of electricity. Imagine what would happen if there were no negative wires in your appliances at home, you'd be waiting a long time for them to work. You see it's a case of taking the positives and the negatives that life throws at you and responding accordingly."

Tom listened, he was surprised and curious that he was having such an in depth conversation with someone he had only just met. "This is all a bit deep isn't it? Why are you telling me this?"

"Because you're listening," said the man.

"OK" said Tom, getting a little irritated. "If you know all the answers what should I be doing to get my life back in balance?"

"Perhaps you ought to ask yourself the same question," said the man gently. "Only you can know how you are out of balance, and only you can know what balance means for you. The starting point is for you to recognise if you feel out of balance. And for you to identify what you need to do to get back into balance."

Tom raised his eyebrows, but before he could speak the man said, "These questions might help."

The man handed Tom a piece of paper. "Find a quiet moment over Christmas to think about them. I suspect you've been ignoring the quiet voice that we each have inside us. The one that knows the answers. When was the last time you had one of those hunches or instincts of what to do next with your life?"

Tom looked puzzled for a moment, as his mind took in the impact of the man's question. "Not for some time," said Tom. "I seem to have lost my spark, that fire that I had at the beginning for doing the right things, making the right decisions. I just seem to be in a rut these days."

"Well, well," said the man smiling back at Tom. "Recognising it is a significant step. These questions will help, but remember to give yourself time to reflect."

Tom looked even more puzzled as the man went on. "You're relying too much on your conscious mind. What about your intuitive mind? Your intuitive mind won't like you rushing around all the time like you have been doing. It will just cause you more stress if you keep doing that."

"It's good that Christmas is here, it'll give you time to reflect while the business is closed. Oh, and don't worry about money, it's sorted, a couple of critical payments are on their way."

"How do you know about the payments situation?" gasped Tom. "You seem to know me and my business, yet we've never met before. At least I don't think so. I came here to rest for a moment, and you turn up giving advice like you know me." Tom was totally puzzled.

The man held up his hand stopping Tom in his tracks. "Oh you know me very well," he said, "and I know you. We haven't talked much recently, but we will." He paused a moment and looked at Tom, "I sense now that you're ready to listen. It's time for a change. That's why it feels like a rut, and that's OK, life sends a signal when things aren't right."

The man smiled, pulled up the collar of his coat and started walking away along the coast path.

"Wait a minute," said Tom. "You said we'd talk some more. How do I get in touch again? What's your name?"

"I'll know when you want to get in touch again," said the man. "There's a lot to discuss. You know where to find me," he said pointing at the bench. "Have a great Christmas, see you in the New Year!"

And with that he was gone, just disappeared into the night, as quickly as he had come.

Tom sat on the bench bewildered by all that had occurred. "It all happened so fast," he said to himself. "How am I going to remember what he said?" Then he recalled the piece of paper in his hand, he unrolled it. On it were written several questions in a distinctive, sloping script:

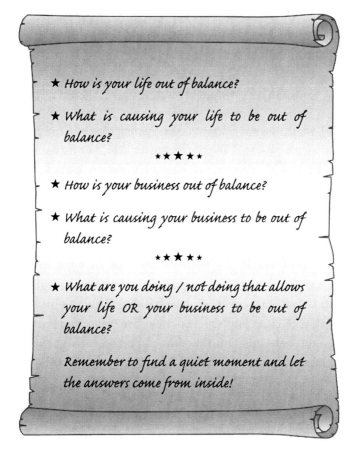

★ *How is your life out of balance?*

★ *What is causing your life to be out of balance?*

★ ★ ★ ★ ★

★ *How is your business out of balance?*

★ *What is causing your business to be out of balance?*

★ ★ ★ ★ ★

★ *What are you doing / not doing that allows your life OR your business to be out of balance?*

Remember to find a quiet moment and let the answers come from inside!

Tom sat for a moment and looked out to sea. "That was the weirdest experience I've ever had," he muttered to himself. He had no idea who the man was. He seemed familiar, yet he couldn't place him. He was like a granddad or a favourite uncle, friendly but wise, with his best interests at heart. And how did he know about the business, the cash flow problem and his own situation? Tom stood up from the bench, it was getting cold now, and it was late. Suzie, his wife, would be wondering where he was. He placed the piece of paper in his pocket and went home more thoughtful than he had been for a long time.

At work the following morning...

When Tom went into work for the half-day of Christmas Eve concern was still niggling away at him, but he couldn't help feeling a glimmer of hope. By eleven o'clock that morning it was confirmed: two payments had been agreed and sent electronically. Tom would cover his commitments. He could relax and enjoy Christmas.

But, how could the man be so sure of what would happen? Just before Tom closed the office for the holiday period, Andrea, one of his staff handed Tom an envelope and said, "A chap popped into the office today and left you this, you were busy on the phone chasing money and he said he didn't want to wait." Andrea paused for a moment fidgeting, as though she wanted to say something else. Tom prompted her saying, "What's the matter Andrea? You look concerned?" Andrea hesitated for a moment, but she just had to ask even if Tom did get annoyed. "Me and the team are concerned about our salaries – they will be OK won't they?"

As Andrea spoke, Tom was opening the envelope and reading the note. It was in the same distinctive handwriting.

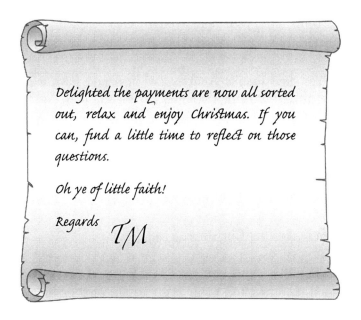

Delighted the payments are now all sorted out, relax and enjoy Christmas. If you can, find a little time to reflect on those questions.

Oh ye of little faith!

Regards TM

Tom stared at the note.

"Something the matter?" asked Andrea.

"Oh, err no, no everything's fine. Don't worry, I've paid your salaries today. Go home, have a great Christmas, and I'll see you all on the 2nd."

The rest of the team had gone to The Marlborough Arms for a Christmas drink. Andrea had promised to have a chat with Tom and then catch them up.

"Are you coming for a drink at The Marlborough?" asked Andrea.

"A drink, oh yes of course, Christmas drink, yes, err no, no, I've got some stuff to sort out here, I'll catch you later."

"Tom, are you sure you're OK?" asked Andrea quizzically.

"Yes, fine thanks Andrea, I'm fine, and have a great Christmas." With that Andrea left for the pub, and Tom sat at his desk, staring at the two pieces of paper in front of him. He assumed the second note was from the man he had met on the bench, he noticed it was signed TM. "Strange" he thought, "he has the same initials as me."Tom needed to think about what was going on.

At home after Christmas...

Christmas came and went in a flurry of presents, too much food and too many visits to family they only saw once a year! Through it all Tom kept thinking back to the strange meeting with the man before Christmas. It didn't make sense to him, but try as he might to dismiss it, something inside him kept thinking that maybe, just maybe he should do as the older guy had suggested and think about those questions.

Then there was the present, that was even harder to explain. How had a present, beautifully wrapped and labelled simply 'To Tom' managed to get under the Christmas tree? His wife swore there hadn't been any strangers in the house and he was sure she and the kids hadn't done it, why would they?

There it had been, a neat little parcel addressed to him. Inside was a book called 'Your Body Speaks Your Mind' by Debbie Shapiro with a card saying 'Merry Christmas,

TM' in the same handwriting, tucked into the section on back pain.

Of course Suzie had wanted to know who the present was from. She wasn't the jealous type, but she was certainly curious. Eventually Tom decided to tell her everything, starting from the impulse to drive to the coast, the meeting on the bench, the deep and meaningful conversation, the note at work and the book. He really hoped that Suzie would find a logical explanation for it all, but instead she seemed really calm and accepting of the whole thing.

She was a bit sceptical at first, but the more he told her about the meeting on the bench, the more enthusiastic she became. "Well everything happens for a reason. Why don't you just accept it and do what he suggests. After all there's no denying that your life is out of balance."

"What do you mean? It's not really out of balance," said Tom half-heartedly.

"If it isn't out of balance, how come you didn't get to any of the kids' school plays this Christmas? You've stopped playing golf with PJ and you and I haven't spent any quality time together for months. The last time we went out was my birthday last February and you even delayed that because of a business meeting. All you think about these days is the business, and you don't even seem to have your old spark and enthusiasm for that," said Suzie.

"Look," she continued, getting exasperated when Tom didn't respond, "this guy has shown up out of the blue, and he's asking questions you need to answer. If you don't slow down soon you'll make yourself ill. People don't just turn up; he must be here for a reason. Why don't you take some time for yourself this afternoon and I'll take the kids out. Go for a walk and see if you can find some answers to his questions?"

Tom thought about it for a few moments and decided he had nothing to lose. Maybe Suzie was right about him being out of balance; certainly everything was getting on top of him at the moment. The more he thought about it, the more he could see what she meant. But at that moment he couldn't begin to see how the business was out of balance.

He spent a good hour trying desperately to figure out what the man meant. He thought back to their conversation on the bench and remembered telling him that he felt he had lost his spark and his knack for doing things right and making the right decisions. What had gone wrong? Was it cash flow? Were they focusing on the customer enough? Or was it the way they were doing their marketing and sales? He kept asking himself more and more questions, until he felt he was going round in circles.

Eventually, he decided to get in the car and go back to the bench by the sailing club. Maybe 'TM' would be there, after all that was where he had said he would be when Tom was ready to talk some more.

So Tom sat and waited. He waited half an hour listening to a voice in his head telling him how stupid he had been for falling for this silly idea. It was ridiculous, the man couldn't possibly know he was there. It wasn't as if he could phone him, or send him a text to say he wanted to meet.

As he went to stand up and walk back to the car, he noticed how beautiful the sea looked in the pale sunlight of a winter's afternoon. The waves were gently lapping on the shore as the gulls wheeled overhead. Into this tranquil silence came an inner voice whispering to him to be still, be quiet and enjoy the moment.

He sat down again on the bench not wanting anything to disturb him.

He wasn't sure how long he'd been sitting there when a voice to his right said, "I see you've been expecting me."

Tom replied, "I didn't think you were coming."

"I told you I'd be here when you were ready," replied the man.

"I've waited over an hour," complained Tom.

"But were you really ready?" asked his companion with a twinkle in his eye. "To find answers you need to be still, not cynical, doubting or impatient."

"I can answer one of the questions," said Tom impatiently. "I mean I can see that I'm out of balance, that's pretty obvious. But the business, what about that?"

The man looked calmly out to sea and said, "Well let's focus on you first. You say that your personal life is out of balance. How do you know?"

"Well other people seem to think I am, for instance my wife says I spend too much time at work, that I'm not spending time with the kids. Then she says I'm putting on weight, not eating well, not playing golf with my best mate, all that kind of stuff."

"Hmmm, so that's what your wife says, but how do you feel about it?"

"She's probably right, I've been feeling that everything's getting on top of me. I'm constantly running around chasing my own tail. But I don't understand what I've got to do about it. I've tried all the usual time management techniques but I still feel hassled as though something is missing."

By way of an answer, the man very pointedly asked Tom a question, in fact he asked Tom for an answer to the same question 6 times: "What's important to you Tom?"

Tom replied "The business."

"What else is important to you?"

"My family."

"What else is important to you?"

"Success."

"What else is important to you?"

"Security."

"What else is important to you?"

"Oh I dunno…. having fun."

He paused before saying finally "Come on, what else is important to you?"

"Mmmmm. …learning?"

Eventually, the man stopped and said, "If all of these things are important to you, are you taking care of each of them appropriately?"

Tom thought for a moment before replying "No."

"Then that's where you're out of balance," replied the man. "Now what about your health, is that important to you?"

"Of course."

"Perhaps you'd better think about that as well. Your health doesn't just look after itself; you need to give your body time to restore itself. You need exercise, relaxation and good food, grabbing a sandwich, as you run for the train doesn't count. After all, you set pretty high standards and demand a lot of yourself," he said knowingly.

"What we've been doing is identifying the things that are important to you about your life in general, these can be regarded as your life values. These dictate how you spend your time and energy. You will have other values for your relationship with Suzie, how you negotiate deals, in fact you'll have values for most things, often without being consciously aware of them."

"If you devote time to your values in a balanced way you feel good about life; if you ignore or act against those values, you're continually dealing with the consequences." He continued, "You'll probably give more energy and time to those values that seem important to you in the moment. Spending more time on your business suggests that the business is more important than your family."

"No it's not," cried Tom horrified.

The man smiled wryly "It's not? I see. So your family is as important to you as your business."

"It's more important," said Tom indignantly.

"Your values affect everything you do and how you do it. Here's an example, if I ask you to do something that is at odds with your values either you won't do it, or you won't do it consistently." The man was looking out to sea, "So you need to consider your values in a wider context, in terms of your direction or purpose in life."

Tom was baffled. The man handed him another piece of carefully rolled paper. He sat in silence whilst Tom read:

★ What is important to you? Once you have your list, describe what you mean by each item.

★ How do you want to be described by others?

★ What activities do you want to do?

★ What do you want to have in your life?

★ What do you want to give back to others?

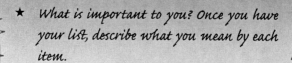

★ What is important to you in terms of your business? Once you have your list, describe what you mean by each item.

★ How do you want the business to be described by others?

★ What activities do you want the business to undertake?

★ What do you want the business to have in terms of its assets?

★ What do you want the business to give back to others?

Tom's immediate reaction was to kick back, "But I haven't answered all the first questions yet, that's why I came to find you. Now you give me another set of questions. I can just about see how to answer them for me personally, but how do they relate to the business?"

The man explained, "How do you want your suppliers, or customers or employees to describe the business? What activities do you want the business to perform? What do you want the business to have – that's all about its assets, revenues and profits? What do you want the business to give back to others is how you want people to benefit from knowing you or dealing with your business. Finally, what is important to you about the business is all about your personal connection with it."

Tom said "OK, so once I've worked out all those questions for myself, and for the business. What then?"

"That's when we have another talk," said the man.

"But I've got a business to run, I haven't time for all this thinking and reflecting."

"Well, you won't find the answers then will you?" replied his mentor.

Tom studied the list of questions, and then turned back. But by then the man had already gone. So Tom kept looking out to sea, thinking about this odd conversation, but more than anything wondering how he could find the time to work through all the questions.

He'd forgotten to ask the man who he was. What was his name? TM. It was a coincidence that his initials were the same as Tom's. He wondered what the T stood for. He certainly didn't look like a Trevor, or Timothy, or even a Tim. He might even be another Tom.

Suddenly, amid all this pondering he remembered his parent's old narrowboat. They hardly ever used it now, and they certainly wouldn't use it at Christmas, but he could. When he and Suzie were dating they used to take it out a lot. He needn't go very far, once he had the stove going the place would soon heat up. If he raided the kitchen cupboards he could pack up a few of his favourite goodies and have some time to himself.

It seemed like a cunning plan to him!

If you would like to explore the concepts covered in this part of the story in more detail go to page 84-95 and read Concepts 1, 2 & 3 or if you prefer, finish the story, and do the exercises at the end.

Chapter 2 – What's most important?

On the narrowboat…

Next morning the ducks woke Tom from a deep sleep and for a moment he couldn't work out where he was. Then it all came back to him. The meeting with the man and the second list of questions. Then going home and telling Suzie he was going away on his own for a couple of days. All this hadn't gone down well in the middle of the Christmas holidays. But Suzie hadn't been able to argue when Tom had reminded her that even she said he hadn't been making enough time for himself recently.

They had talked about the man. They had speculated about who he might be and how they came to meet on the seat. Then there were his initials – TM – they couldn't figure it out from that either.

Whoever the man was, Tom had decided to take his advice, and he had stuck to his decision to spend a couple of days on the narrow boat. First he had raided the fridge for something more exciting than cold turkey; he grabbed a few bottles of his favourite beer, and finally headed over to his parents to pick up the keys to the boat. His mum had fretted about it being cold and damp, but once the fire was going and the doors were closed on the outside world it was really warm and cosy and he had packed his warm clothing just in case it got really cold!

Now he was awake, he realised if he stayed in the marina there would be lots of interruptions. Old Ken who owned the place always wanted to chat! So he headed up stream to a quiet spot near one of his favourite real ale pubs. After all, he had been firmly told to relax as well as find some quiet time for himself.

By late afternoon he had worked his way through most of the questions. He was starting to see how much he had let his whole life get out of balance. He decided it was time to get out the torch, put on his wellies and stroll up to the pub for an early supper.

An hour later he felt much more content sitting by a roaring fire, a pint of the landlord's finest ale in front of him, gazing into the flames. Suddenly a voice beside him said, "This is the life!"

Tom's eyes almost popped out of his head. He'd wondered if he would meet 'the man on the bench', but to see him sitting in the pub was astounding. In a split second Tom realised it was more about his state of mind, which dictated when his new found mentor appeared. Tom felt relaxed, he'd let go and he was enjoying himself.

He didn't reply immediately, he continued staring into the fire.

Eventually Tom said, "Yes, you're right, this is the life. I realise that I haven't been spending enough time on my own relaxing or reflecting. Someone always seems to want me, either the business, or the kids, or Suzie, or my parents. I just seem to be reacting all the time. I hardly ever think about what I'm doing or why I'm doing it. This last 24 hours has been great, I feel I can see my whole life much more clearly. That's obviously going to be better not just for me, but for everyone else around me."

"I can see now why there's so much hassle at work. I'm snapping at the team and they're snapping back at me. I suppose you know that my PA, Bev, left a few months ago. She was brilliant; I could trust her to do anything. All of a sudden she said she'd found a new job. At the time I couldn't understand why she was going – she even went to a place where the pay was less. She said when she started working for me there was a really clear vision. And she knew she was part of it. Apparently that wasn't the case in the end so she found a new job. Now I can see what she meant."

The man said "It must have been really frustrating for her, seeing you lose your direction. She might have been feeling less valued and important if you weren't sharing your plans anymore."

"Yes," agreed Tom. "I can see that now. In fact I think I need to get right back to work and sort this mess out. I've got a good team, but I can see they aren't getting the leadership they need from me. I'll spend tonight on the boat then I'll head back and get into the office tomorrow afternoon. That way I can spend a couple of days putting my plans together before the team get back after New Year."

"Hold on a minute," said the man in a quiet voice. "What about your home life? Isn't that still a tiny bit out of balance?"

Tom thought for a minute, in his heart he knew the man was right, but somehow the home stuff seemed harder to fix. Suzie was trying to be supportive, but he knew how snappy she was getting and he knew that under the surface things weren't as good as they had been between them.

But he couldn't stop himself from saying "Why do I need to think about my home life first? I can see what I need to do with the business, surely if I sort that out first, then I'll have more time for thinking about the family."

"Well," replied the man, "it all depends on what's most important to you. Start by addressing the things that matter most to you, then support the other things you come to consider."

"When we met on the bench I asked what was important to you. The things you said were the business, your family, success, security, having fun, learning and then you added in your health as an after-thought. Now what you need to do is rank those in order."

"Well the top three are my family, my health and my business. And they're pretty much in that order," said Tom. "Then I think it's security, learning and success. I think having fun is important though, it's just I used to apply it to everything I did, whilst recently the fun's been missing.

I can see that now. Wouldn't it be great if it could all be fun again."

"Indeed, indeed," said the man with a knowing glint in his eye. "Now can you see why it's important to sort out family and health issues before you focus on the business? They're most important to you, you've just said so. Give them priority. With family and health in balance you'll be able to make better decisions for your business."

The man continued, "So your family is number one. What exactly do you mean by family and how are they important to you?"

"Well that's obvious," replied Tom. "It's Suzie and the kids."

"Oh right," said the man. "And would Suzie agree with that?"

Tom reflected for a moment, and then replied "She'd include her Mum as well, and her brother Alexander in New Zealand. Not to mention my Mum and Dad, how could I forget them!"

"When something's important to us it's good to be really clear about what we mean by it. On the first list of questions I suggested you write down the things that were important to you, and what you meant by them. Did you do that?"

"No," replied Tom. "At the time I thought it was obvious, but I see what you mean now. It's like giving each value a definition so it's clear in my own mind. That's what you mean isn't it?"

"That's it exactly," said the man. "Also it'll help when you talk about your values with other people. You see they may think of family as something different again." He paused then went on "Now we know what you mean by the family, tell me what's important to you about it."

"It's important to me that we have fun together, that I spend time playing with the kids and that Suzie and I have some time on our own. But as Suzie keeps reminding me, none of that is happening at the moment."

"Do you have any goals for that?" asked the man.

"What do you mean? I don't think I set goals for anything, unless you mean the target I set for the business each year in terms of turnover, and to be honest that's not really a goal, just a number the accountant and the bank manager talk about!"

His companion wasn't surprised by Tom's response. From all he knew about Tom, he was well aware that goals and planning were fundamentally lacking from his life. Trying to be helpful he said "Do you remember I asked you about how you want to be described by others, what activities you want to do, what you want to have in your life and what you want to give back to others."

Tom reflected for a minute, and then he said, "You're right. I used to plan more, especially around making time for the family." He added in a somewhat dejected tone "I don't even find the time to play golf with my best mate anymore."

Ignoring the note of self-pity in Tom's voice the man said, "So while you're still on the narrowboat with time to think clearly without interruptions, I suggest you mull over this." He handed Tom another piece of paper.

Last time you identified your purpose and what was important to you, what activities you want to do, how you want to be described, what you want, and what to give back to others. So, now using this:

★ Identify three tasks or goals you could complete which would take you closer what you described.

★ Create a plan by answering the following questions:

  ☆ Does achieving this goal take you closer to your purpose?

  ☆ What could get in the way of you achieving this goal?

  ☆ What resources do you need?

  ☆ What tasks need to be completed to achieve the goal?

  ☆ Who could help you and how?

  ☆ How will you measure completion?

  ☆ How will you celebrate completion?

★ Decide what to tackle first and then make a start.

Tom glanced over the questions before turning to look at the man, but of course, he had already gone. Tom remained sitting by the fireside gazing into the flames, thinking about how to get his life back on course.

On the boat, Tom spent much of the following day working through the tasks. It surprised him how much he enjoyed it. In a small way he was actually having fun! In the afternoon he cruised back to the marina and headed for home. He felt more comfortable with himself than he had done for a long time and he was longing to talk to Suzie about all his thoughts, ideas and plans.

The next few weeks...

Suzie was really supportive. She was absolutely delighted when he said he was actually going to make time to be with the family and look after his own health. They even decided to crack open the bottle of Champagne they'd saved for New Year's Eve.

After New Year Tom went back to work. He was fired up and enthusiastic. Everyone noticed how much more focused he was. He was trying to make work more fun, because in one of his eureka moments on the boat, he'd come to the conclusion that 'a happy office is a productive office'. Above all he was making more time for himself and the family. Lunch wasn't just a sandwich 'on the run' anymore and at least three times a week he was leaving the office in time to see the twins before they went to bed.

It was going really well until mid-January. Tom had planned to take Suzie out for supper one evening. He'd booked a table at the Italian restaurant in the village and Suzie's mum was going to baby-sit. Then at the last minute something had come up at work and he had to stay late.

He'd rung Suzie to say he would be late home as soon as he'd realised. When he eventually got home Suzie was furious. She completely lost her temper and brought up all the stuff that had been annoying her for months….you never do this, you promised to do that…she went on for ages. In the end she'd stormed out saying she was going 'out' and he could look after the kids for a change.

Her parting words were "I've supported you for years while you worked on your precious business. I put up with all this stuff about this supposed man on the bench. I let you go off on your own at Christmas. You came back with all those plans and promises, but nothing's changed. As soon as something happens at the office, it's always more important than me and the kids!"

As he turned round from the slamming front door, he had to admit to himself that most of what she'd said was true. He was just replaying it in his mind when he noticed the children peering from behind the playroom door. The twin boys looked like they were about to burst into tears. His daughter a couple of years older looked ready to continue where her mother had finished! He had that familiar sinking feeling and the realisation that yet again fun had flown out of the window.

Eventually, the children were all bathed and in bed, although none of them had wanted to go to sleep without saying goodnight to Mummy. The irony of the fact that they often went to bed without saying goodnight to Daddy was not lost on Tom.

Once all three were sound asleep, Tom looked at the chaos surrounding him in the playroom, lounge and bathroom. The prospect of bringing the house back to some sense of normality before Suzie's return was daunting. He needed a breath of fresh air, and a moment or two to think.

Standing on the patio, looking up at the stars, wondering how it had all gone wrong, he noticed a light on in the summerhouse. He immediately thought it was Suzie, so he headed across the garden ready with his excuses and explanations. He was startled, it wasn't Suzie; his mysterious mentor was sitting on a garden chair looking for all the world as though he belonged there.

"Hello," said the man. "What a lovely summer house, these cushions and curtains are really pretty. Did Suzie make them?"

The twinkle of mischief in the man's eye was lost on Tom as he retorted, "Don't talk to me about Suzie. She's just stormed out leaving me to look after the kids. I don't know where she's gone or when she's coming back. I've tried to ring her three times, she must have turned her phone off."

His mentor asked what had happened, and Tom started explaining about the planned evening out and his delay at the office.

"OK, so you made a commitment and then something else cropped up?"

"Yes that's right."

"Was it more important than taking Suzie out as you had promised?"

"Of course it was. It was urgent!" exclaimed Tom.

"I didn't ask if it was more urgent," said the man. "I asked if it was more important. There's a big difference between what's urgent and what's important. Urgent stuff is linked to time – it has to happen today, this minute or now, that's urgent. Important is linked to consequences and is likely to be directly linked to your values."

He went on "You told me your family was more important to you than your business, but your actions appear to show that your business is more important than your family. That's why Suzie is so annoyed and upset."

Tom thought about it for a moment, then he said "But the thing that happened at the office needed sorting out tonight. It was really urgent."

"OK, so if it was really urgent, could someone else have dealt with it? What about Andrea?"

"Well I suppose she could have done it. She would've had to if I hadn't been in the office this afternoon."

"One day, we'll have a chat about delegating," said the man. "But we'll leave that for another day. Right now Suzie's the focus. If you make a commitment and break it, eventually people stop forgiving you. Whether it's a personal relationship or a business relationship, you still have to work at it. Relationships are all about give and take, you have to put back in, as well as taking out."

He went on "How are you going to show Suzie how much she means to you and start putting something back?"

"I don't know," said Tom. "We used to love going to London for a couple of days, see a show, do some shopping and sightseeing, that sort of thing. Suzie really used to enjoy that although we haven't done it since the kids came along."

"The trouble is getting a babysitter. Suzie's mum is ideal but she works at the weekend, so it would need to be during the week and that means leaving the office. I haven't left the team on their own for a whole day, never mind two since Bev left."

"I thought you said you had a good team," said the man.

"Well I have," said Tom reflectively. "Maybe you're right, maybe it is time I left them on their own. Andrea's been with me long enough; I ought to trust her by now. She can always call my mobile if she has a problem."

"Don't you think Suzie would feel better if you told her you were going to turn your phone off? After all, if there's a problem with the children, her mum can call Suzie's mobile. That way you probably won't be interrupted at all."

Of course, Tom could see the sense of it. "Suzie will feel special if we have a whole two days together without phone calls from the office – and it's what we both deserve. All I have to do is find her and ask for a second chance."

"OK, OK It's a bit more than my second chance," he said in response to the man's raised eyebrow. "Suzie really matters to me and I want her to know that."

He turned to see if the man had any more to say, but he'd already gone. Where the man had been sitting was a piece of paper:

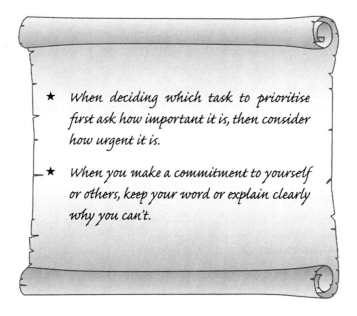

★ When deciding which task to prioritise first ask how important it is, then consider how urgent it is.

★ When you make a commitment to yourself or others, keep your word or explain clearly why you can't.

If you would like to explore the concepts covered in this part of the story in more detail go to page 98-109 and read Concepts 4, 5 & 6 or if you prefer, finish the story, and do the exercises at the end.

Chapter 3 – You can't do it all on your own

Some weeks later...

Tom was sitting on a train coming back from a review meeting with one of their best customers. The meeting had gone really well and they were expecting to get even more work from them.

As he thought back over the meeting, he started reflecting on all the other good things that had happened since Christmas. Of course there was all the stuff with 'the man on the bench' and the night Suzie had walked out. But then there was the great break he and Suzie had shared in London. It had been so good to spend time with her. They had really enjoyed the show and it had been so long since they had spent time on their own together, he had even found the obligatory shopping trip fun! Above all they had talked far more openly and honestly than they had for years – probably since their first child was born.

During their trip to London they'd started speculating about 'the man on the bench'. They'd weighed up the facts; his initials were TM, he seemed to know Tom well and he had an uncanny knack for appearing in just the right place at the moment he was needed. When Tom tried to explain to Suzie the way the man appeared and disappeared into thin air, Suzie jokingly said he sounded like a magician. And it was several hours later, that she'd suddenly exclaimed,

"You know, TM could stand for "The Magician", that's what I'm going to call him."

During that couple of days Tom had reflected quite a lot about "The Magician" – the name had of course stuck. He was loath to admit it, but he felt that in some way his new found mentor had been having quite a magical effect on him.

He understood now what Suzie had meant about feeling that she was always in second place to the business. The Magician had sent him another book – this one had been neatly wrapped in brown paper and placed under his pillow of all places! It was called 'The 7 Habits of Highly Effective People' by Stephen Covey. It had lots in it about identifying what's important and what's urgent, but The Magician had tagged the part about relationships and how to think of them as bank accounts. You can make deposits and you can make withdrawals, but if you make too many withdrawals there is nothing left to take out.

He could see now that he had been like that with Suzie, she had supported him so much, he had drawn on her much more than was fair. Now he was really starting to repay that debt and investing in the relationship to make it work better for both of them. That felt good.

Another thing that was working well was spending more time with the kids. They were growing up fast; he wanted to make the most of his time with them. Also he was seeing his old friend PJ, for a regular game of golf. He'd hardly seen PJ for months, and was feeling a bit guilty about how many games he'd cancelled. Now Tom was determined to keep his personal commitments as well as his business commitments, especially to the people who were important to him. That certainly had to include PJ, he was his best mate and they'd been at school together.

He hadn't intended to tell PJ about The Magician, but somehow it had slipped out one day. He'd ended up telling him the whole story. Far from being sceptical, PJ had laughed out loud and said, "So you've got your very own wise man." Tom had asked what he meant and PJ had said "Why do you think I hardly ever miss my game of golf. I wouldn't be without my 'Very Wise Man', I always ask myself what would VWM say, when I'm not sure what to do."

As Tom was happily reflecting on magicians and wise men a voice beside him said "So life with Suzie and the kids is back on track. And you're starting to make PJ work hard to beat you on the golf course. But how are your relationships doing at work?"

Tom realised The Magician was sitting in the empty seat beside him, though whether he was visible to anyone else in the compartment, Tom wasn't so sure. Either way he couldn't stop himself from replying indignantly, "What do you mean? My relationships at work are fine, and I've just got lots more business from an existing customer."

"If you've got such good relationships, why didn't you delegate that job that needed doing last week?"

"Well," replied Tom. "If Bev had been here she could've done it, but she wasn't."

"So what about Andrea?"

"I'm just not sure about Andrea," said Tom.

"Is that because of the upset you had with her last week?" asked The Magician. "Oh yes, I know about that. Andrea getting annoyed about how you never trust her to develop the business and you getting defensive saying that you do trust her to get on with things it's just that you need to know everything that's going on."

"Well it's true," said Tom. "For the last couple of years things have really been very tight. It's doing better at the moment, but that's only the last two or three months – well since Christmas. I still can't afford for anything to go wrong."

"So does that mean that you employ people to do a job and then chase round after them to such an extent that you might as well have done the job yourself; whilst the person you employed feels like she's 'an overpaid office junior'? Wasn't that the phrase Andrea used? How are you ever going to grow the business any further if you don't trust any of your people?"

"Well I do trust Andrea, it's just..." Tom paused for a moment reflecting. "Well I'm not sure what it is. But sometimes I give her things to do, but she doesn't quite do them right."

"Do you always give her clear instructions?" The Magician replied.

"She can work it out," said Tom.

"Maybe she can't," continued The Magician. "You see, when it comes to delegating a task, it isn't as simple as people sometimes think. If you want something done a certain way, you need to be clear with your communication. You need to check the other person understands, then you need to keep communicating with them and be available to support when they need you."

The Magician paused before continuing, "If you do it properly, delegating is a great deal more than just getting rid of a task. Effective delegation is more rewarding for both you and the person you delegate to."

Tom thought for a moment, and then said, "I must have delegated to Bev, but I didn't even think about it. She just seemed to read my mind and know what needed to be done and more importantly how I wanted it doing."

"Bev began working for you as soon as you started the business, so she knew everything that was going on. In the early days she was part of every decision you made, so it was easy for her to see what needed doing. And you spent a lot of time talking about your hopes and dreams for the business, so she knew your values and what was important to you."

"Yes," said Tom. "I suppose she did. I'd never thought of it like that before." Then he asked, "So what do I need to do about Andrea, because you're right, I do trust her, it's just that I find it difficult not to control everything."

"Well firstly, can you think of a task that you can give Andrea to do? Something important so that it shows how much you trust her, but also something that she's going to enjoy doing, and has the skills, knowledge and experience to do."

Tom thought for a moment, then said "She could organise our next big trade exhibition. That's really important for the business, but it's also something that she enjoys and she's fully involved with. In fact, if I call her and tell her now, she can go to the meeting I've arranged next week with the people who design our stand."

With that Tom reached over to pick up his mobile phone. Before he touched the first number, The Magician said quietly "Don't you think we need to consider this a little more before you throw this major project over to Andrea without so much as a backward glance?"

"What do you mean? I just need to tell her she can manage the whole of the exhibition this year, and I trust her to do a good job, don't I?"

"Consider for a moment how Andrea will feel when you tell her that. Don't you think she'll feel it's a knee-jerk reaction to what she said last week? Do you really think she'll trust you not to come back in a few days time demanding to know what she's done and instructing her to do everything the way you like it?"

The Magician went on, "It's like your relationships with your family and PJ. You need to build mutual trust. Andrea has to know that you will keep your word and that you will do what you say you will. She also needs to know that you trust her. When this happens she'll feel empowered and start being more proactive and self-reliant. Until then, you and she are going to have to work at building up your relationship."

Tom replied "So you mean it's a bit like my relationship with Suzie, only this time I need to talk to Andrea and understand what's important to her."

"That's the idea," said The Magician. "Then develop a bit of a plan for how you can hand over more responsibility to her, but step by step over time. Don't try to change overnight – that won't work for either of you. Start with one project, and make sure that Andrea is comfortable with what you want her to do, and how much she needs to report back to you. Also let her know that you'll be there to provide guidance and support if she needs it, but only if she asks."

Tom sat back in his seat thinking, and then he said, "If Andrea really does look after all the exhibition stuff, that would free a big chunk of my time. I could even get onto chasing a bit more business, I've got loads of warm leads I haven't had chance to contact recently."

He looked round to see what The Magician thought of that idea, only to find that not only had The Magician apparently disappeared into thin air again, but that the train was pulling into his station.

Back at the office....

Tom went to call Andrea in to see him. He had decided to delegate the exhibition to Andrea, assuming that she wanted to do it. On his way to Andrea's desk he found himself thinking about how annoyed he would be if someone interrupted him while he was in the middle of something else. So instead he spoke to Andrea quietly for a few minutes, explaining that he had been thinking about what Andrea had said the previous week and wanted to discuss how they could work together differently. They agreed to meet the following day and set a good hour aside for their talk. Tom really surprised Andrea by saying he would ensure they had no interruptions.

The meeting started well. Andrea responded with a genuine enthusiasm to Tom's obvious attempt to put things right. She appreciated Tom taking the time to find out about her values and what mattered to her.

They had always had quite a good relationship until the last year or so. It was after Bev had left when Tom started micro-managing things. So perhaps Tom shouldn't have been surprised when Andrea tentatively said "It's great that you've started talking to me more, and giving me a bit more responsibility, but what about the rest of the team?"

Tom was quiet for a moment as Andrea carried on, "I mean, you used to have time for people, but now it feels like you're checking up on us all the time. You seem always to be dashing from one thing to the next. Poor Carla doesn't know whether she's on her head or her heels. It was alright taking her on to replace Bev, but we all know she's not up to that; she's a good administrator, but she needs a bit of guidance from you. At the moment she's spending half her time wondering what you want her to do next, and the other half terrified that she's not doing what you want her to do."

She paused for a moment and Tom thought she'd finished, but then Andrea said something that really hit home, "I bet you don't even really know why Bev left."

"Well she found another job," Tom replied lamely.

"Yes, but why did she even start looking? That's the question," said Andrea. "And I'll tell you the answer because no one else will. It's because you stopped talking to her, she didn't know what you wanted anymore and she stopped feeling valued and trusted. Everyone who's been here since the early days is feeling like that, it's just Bev had the sense to do something about it, rather than sitting around and grumbling like the others."

Tom said, as much to himself as to Andrea, "Do you think I should be sitting down with everyone, talking to them all one-to-one like this?"

"Yep. Mind you, they'll all be wondering what's come over you, but if you do it right, I think it would do more for productivity than a pay rise" replied Andrea.

That made Tom smile. Then he started to look worried as he thought of how much time it would all take. Suddenly his face broke into a broad grin as he remembered that he'd just delegated the big exhibition to Andrea, so he finished the meeting saying, "You'd better make a good job of organising the exhibition. That'll give me the time to talk to all the team and get some more new business as well!"

Over the next couple of weeks, Tom made the time to talk to all his staff. The business was still small enough that this was realistic. He sat down with each of them, getting them thinking about their values and what's important to them. He helped them with agreeing their expectations and talking about their role.

Suddenly, before he knew where he was it was Easter and the big exhibition was the following week. Andrea had done such a good job organising it that Tom had almost forgotten it was happening.

It went exceptionally well. Andrea had introduced a couple of new ideas that Tom hadn't thought of and there were a good number of genuine enquiries. All in all business was booming.

But during May pressure was building and Tom was really challenged to stay on top of things. One Friday evening Andrea popped her head round Tom's door. "I'm off now," she said. "Have a good weekend."

A harassed Tom looked up and snapped, "How can I have a good weekend with all I've still got to do. I think I'll have to cancel my golf with PJ, and I certainly don't feel like going out to dinner with Suzie tonight. There's so much going on I just can't keep up."

"Is there anything I can do to help?" asked Andrea.

As Tom shook his head dejectedly Andrea said, "You know the way you've been today, you'll soon be acting like you were before Christmas. The last few months have been great, until we got so busy. What's the difference?"

"I don't know," said Tom. Then he added with the suggestion of a smile, "but I bet I know a man who does."

"What?" asked Andrea mystified.

"Oh you've just set me thinking about something that's all. You go and have a good weekend, and hopefully I'll have sorted myself out before Monday."

"I hope so, for your sake as much as for mine and the rest of the team's," replied Andrea.

As Andrea left the office, Tom reached for the phone to call Suzie. He hadn't cancelled one of their evenings out together since their trip to London. He thought tonight she would understand and he was right. She understood that he needed to talk to The Magician. In fact she'd been going to suggest it to him when they went out for dinner!

He looked at all the unfinished stuff on his desk and his laptop, and he paused to think about whether it was urgent or important and decided it could all wait until Monday. Andrea's comment made Tom realise it was important for himself and everyone around him, to get himself back into balance.

With that, he drove over to Bosmouth's Sailing Club and walked towards his favourite bench. As he approached he couldn't help feeling a bit disappointed, someone was already sitting on it. He decided to walk onto the next seat, hoping that The Magician would still appear.

As he walked past a voice from the bench said, "I got your message, what's the problem?"

Tom looked round and realised The Magician was already sitting in their favourite spot. Dejectedly Tom sat down beside him "I've done all you suggested, my relationships are better, business is booming, but I feel like I'm being pulled in all directions again. I just can't keep all of my commitments and do everything I need to do."

"You're absolutely right," agreed The Magician.

"What do you mean, I'm right! That's no help to me; I came to see you because I need to know how to get back into balance."

"So," said The Magician, "'if you did know what you needed to do, what would it be?"

Tom thought for a moment, before saying "Well I need to stop doing something. But what?"

The Magician looked out to the clear blue sea and said, "So far you've been delegating individual tasks, but you haven't yet delegated control or responsibility. What you've done, has allowed your team to feel more trusted and empowered. Now they're probably ready and willing to go further. It's time for you to delegate even more, including some of the things you enjoy."

Tom was still looking puzzled, so The Magician gave a couple of examples. "You know Andrea made a good job of that exhibition, why not get her to look after all your exhibitions, including deciding which ones to attend and which ones to miss for the next year. And how about giving Carla more control of your accounts? You know she used to do that in her old job, she told you when you had your one-to-one meeting."

"I suppose I could," said Tom. "I hadn't thought of it like that before. I know I can trust them because they've done all the tasks that I've asked them to, or they've come back to me if they didn't know how to do something."

"That's it. They trust you and you trust them, you've created an atmosphere of mutual trust. Now you can really start to delegate," said The Magician. Then he added, "Of course some time soon we need to think about 'setting objectives for the whole team, by the whole team,' but we're not quite ready for that yet. Well I must be off."

Tom smiled at The Magician and said "Aren't you going to give me a piece of paper now, with my next task on it?"

"Well since you mention it, I do have a piece of paper for you."

"But this is blank," said Tom as he took the proffered piece of paper.

"Don't you think you can write your own instructions this time?"

"Well I suppose so," replied Tom, searching his pockets for a pen. He didn't bother looking towards The Magician after that, he was getting a pretty good idea of when he would appear and disappear.

He pondered a while and then wrote the list of what he needed to do next:

Look at the relationships around you:

★ What are their expectations of you?

★ What are your expectations of them?

For each relationship ask:

★ What's important to you about our relationship?

★ How will you work together?

Look at all the tasks you are currently doing and that need doing.

★ Decide which you can delegate.

★ Think who has the skills to do each task, whether they understand the task and what support they will need.

★ Think about how long it will take to fully delegate responsibility to them.

★ Is the relationship strong enough to make this agreement?

★ Start delegating!

As Tom stood up and turned to walk back to his car and head for home, he reflected on the fact that The Magician had completely delegated the task of writing the note. "Very clever" he said to himself " I must remember that one!"

If you would like to explore the concepts covered in this part of the story in more detail go to page 110-121 and read Concepts 7, 8 & 9 or if you prefer, finish the story, and do the exercises at the end.

Chapter 4 – The turning point

A couple of months later....

It was July and Tom's life was going really well. He had delegated more tasks and the team was responding well. In fact the business was doing so well they had just recruited two new staff, Zeb and Chris. At home, Suzie and the kids seemed to be content and he was spending much more time with them. He was also making time for his weekly golf match with PJ. All in all he felt pretty good about things.

He was reflecting on all of this late one Tuesday afternoon when he was interrupted by the ring of the telephone. It was Darren, the senior manager for one of their best customers. Darren wanted to arrange a meeting to discuss a great new business opportunity. Tom's company had been working closely with two of their regional offices for several years. Now Darren said their board of directors was so impressed with what Tom's firm were doing, they wanted Tom to take on the contract for all their offices. That would be twelve regional offices covering the whole country!

As he put the phone down, Tom was punching the air with delight. He couldn't believe that such a great opportunity had come to them, completely out of the blue. He would never have expected this customer to consider placing such a big contract with a small company like theirs.

Tom went into the main office to share the news with Andrea but she was out at a customer meeting. He wanted to tell Andrea first because she was the person who dealt with this customer on a day-to-day basis, so it was really her hard work that had brought this about. Carla said she wasn't coming back to the office that day, so Tom decided to go home early and share the news with Suzie instead.

Driving home Tom was having second thoughts. A game of tennis was going on in his head. One side was thinking about the great contract and the increase in turnover. The other side was worrying about whether they could cope with it and would it be profitable. Add to that, the client wanted them to do some work that was entirely new to Tom's team. That would take them well out of their comfort zone.

It was all going round and round in his head as he pulled into the driveway and the twins came running out to meet him. These days he did sometimes come home early and surprise them all, but it was still a treat for Daddy to be home before the twins had their tea.

Tom played with the kids for a while trying to enjoy the simple pleasures of family life, but all the time he was thinking about the phone call. The more he thought about it, the more he wasn't sure whether they could do the contract or not.

Eventually Suzie said, "What's wrong?"

"Nothing, I'm fine," replied Tom.

"No you're not. I know you too well, I can tell when you're having one of your 'in your cave' moments. What's the matter?"

So Tom told Suzie all about the phone call and what a great business opportunity it was. She was delighted. She didn't see a problem until he told her about the doubts that he was having and how he couldn't see what to do.

"I'd like to take some time out to think about it, and work through a plan. Maybe go to the narrowboat at the weekend and see if I can talk to The Magician. The problem is I told Darren I'd give him an answer in principle by the end of the week. We agreed we'd keep it just between ourselves until I've decided if it's something we're going to go for."

Suzie said, "Well why don't you go to the narrowboat tomorrow or Thursday and leave Andrea to cover for you?"

"But I can't just leave her with my meetings and stuff without any warning."

"Why not? Surely you trust her enough to do that. Especially if it's only for a day."

Tom thought for a moment. "Well I certainly trust her to do it. But usually if I'm out for a day we talk through what I need her to do the night before." He mulled it over a little more. "Yes, you're right, I've only got one meeting and I know

Andrea can handle that. I can go over to the narrowboat first thing and call her from there to let her know."

The following day....

Tom called Andrea from the narrowboat and explained that he was leaving her in charge for the day as he needed a bit of thinking time. Andrea was more than a bit surprised because it was something Tom had never done without warning before. But once Tom convinced her nothing was wrong and that he just wanted a bit of thinking time, Andrea agreed that she could handle anything that happened.

With that Tom left the marina and headed up stream avoiding a chat with old Ken. He moored up under a willow tree, made a cup of coffee and sat on the back of the boat waiting for The Magician to appear. Time went on and there was no sign of him. Tom started to get agitated and drum his fingers on the cabin roof. He couldn't understand why The Magician wasn't appearing. He needed his help right now.

Eventually, he gave up waiting and decided to carry on up stream towards the pub. If nothing else, he thought he might as well have a nice lunch rather than feel the day was a complete waste.

He started to relax and enjoy the day. His hand was on the tiller, the sun was warming his arm, and he saw a heron suddenly take off from the reeds. Just as he was thinking that really life wasn't bad at all, a voice from the tow path interrupted him.

"Lovely morning. I said you needed to relax if you wanted to talk to me."

Tom looked round, almost annoyed that his lovely interlude had been disturbed. But he had the grace to smile, after all this was what he had wanted. So he pulled into the bank and made to moor up, but The Magician said, "Why don't we just carry on up stream a little way? As you've realised it's a lovely morning for cruising along."

"OK," said Tom and The Magician climbed aboard. They sat companionably enjoying the sights and sounds of the river. It reminded Tom of summer holidays when he was a child.

Eventually The Magician broke the silence, "Why did you want to talk to me? Is it that call you got yesterday afternoon?"

"Yes," said Tom. "It sounds a wonderful opportunity, but I'm not sure that we can handle all that extra business at the moment."

When Tom had told him about all the exciting possibilities, as well as his concerns The Magician said, "So it's a business situation and it will impact on the whole team if you go for it."

"Yes," replied Tom.

"So what do the team think about it?"

"I don't know. I haven't told them about it yet."

His mentor sat back and took a deep breath, "So you've been doing all this work developing the team, but you still haven't got to the stage where you're involving them in decisions about the business?"

"Well no," replied Tom. "Do you think I should?"

"Look at it this way. If you involve them more, they'll develop a sense of ownership and be keener to work together as a team to make things happen."

"I'd never thought of it like that," said Tom. "I suppose it's just a logical extension of the way that I've been involving them individually in specific areas of the business."

"That's right. Now it's time to start getting them involved in seeing the bigger picture, the more strategic stuff."

"But it's still my business."

"Of course it is. But they're the team who make things happen and they'll have lots of bright ideas of their own. After all the business is their livelihood too. They want it to succeed just as much as you."

Tom thought for a moment and then said, "So this business proposition I've got, you think I should ask the team whether they think we should take it on. And then get their ideas about how we make it happen."

"Absolutely Tom, but there's another thing you need to think about first – the strategic direction of the business. Do you really know where the business is headed?"

"I haven't had time to think about that for a while. It was difficult to keep the business going last year, and this year we've been getting busier and busier. Should I be involving the whole team in thinking about our strategic direction as well?"

"What feels right to you?" asked The Magician.

"Of course I should. I knew that as soon as I'd asked the question. Why is it these things are so obvious when you're here but I don't think about them otherwise?"

"Well perhaps you still don't always give yourself enough time to relax and step back from the day-to-day 'busy-ness' of life. But we can talk about that another time. Right now what you need to do is fill a few pieces of paper with your next tasks." With that he handed Tom a whole sheaf of blank paper.

Tom said "Does this take me back to your original set of questions that I couldn't understand? You know, when you asked me how I wanted our suppliers, or customers or employees to describe the business? And what activities I wanted the business to perform? And what I wanted the business to have in terms of assets and stuff, as well as what I wanted the business to give back?" Then he added as an afterthought, "Oh and what's important to me about the business?"

"That's the idea," said The Magician. "But there's also another bit to add to that. You also need the team to agree the way they work together. If you think back you've asked people individually what's important to them. Now is the time to ask them collectively what's important to them in terms of how they work together as a team."

"Why's that?" asked Tom.

"Doing that will help you set the rules and guidelines for how you work together. It will become more important as the team grows, especially if you go for this opportunity. It'll mean a lot of hard work and a few frayed tempers over the next months. They need to know what to expect from each other as well as from you."

The Magician went on "If you think about it, six months ago you couldn't even have contemplated this contract. There were too many tensions between different people in the team, now they work much better together and their relationships with you are far better, which is helping everyone."

Tom looked at the blank pieces of paper in his hand, "Do I need to think of the answers beforehand, or do I just call a meeting and go into it with a blank sheet of paper and no pre-conceived ideas."

"Well," came the answer. "It is your business, but there's a difference between having pre-conceived answers and being well prepared to facilitate a meeting that might come up with some ideas even you haven't thought of!"

"Alright," said Tom. "I get the message. After we've thought about the business direction and how we work together, then we go on to think about this new business opportunity. Is that it?"

"Absolutely. Once you've clearly defined the business purpose and values, then you can properly evaluate any opportunity that comes along. By asking yourselves how it helps you to move towards your goal or away from it you can decide whether to pursue it or not."

Tom watched a family of ducks paddling by in a line as he spoke, "My only problem is, how am I going to get the whole team together and do all of this as well as our current work in time to get back to the customer by the end of the week?"

"Tom, this is an important decision for you. Remember the difference between urgent and important?"

"Of course I do," replied Tom. "It's just that I like to get back to people quickly and I don't always stop to think things through."

The Magician chuckled at Tom's growing awareness of his own shortcomings, "Well, what I suggest you do is to phone your customer and explain that this is an important decision so you'd like an extra week to think it through and analyse the potential and develop a plan. Chances are they'll be impressed that you're taking this seriously. Not jumping at a big piece of business without considering the implications for your staff and other customers."

Tom could see that made sense and agreed he would phone Darren later that afternoon to run it by him.

Then he looked down at the sheaf of paper, he counted out a page for each of the team. "Why have I got four sheets left over? It's not like you to be inaccurate."

"There's more than one team in your life that'll be affected by this," said The Magician.

"You mean I need to do the same with Suzie?"

"Ideally you should involve the children a little as well. After all if you take on this contract you won't be home early for a while, and you'll be working more than a few late nights and maybe the occasional weekend. If you involve the family in the decision making process they can agree the tradeoffs with you, like maybe taking a longer family holiday when the contract's up and running."

"Brilliant," said Tom, "that's really helped me see how to take this forward." He turned round to suggest that they have lunch together, but he found himself alone.

He wrote quickly on the pieces of paper while The Magician's ideas were still clear in his mind....

Meet with the team and ask:

★ What is important to you in terms of the business? Once you have your list describe what you mean by each item.

★ How do you want the business to be described by others?

★ What activities do you want the business to undertake?

★ What do you want the business to have in terms of its assets?

★ What do you want the business to give back to others?

★ What is important to the team in terms of how they work together?

★ What are the teams top priorities? – Plan them in!

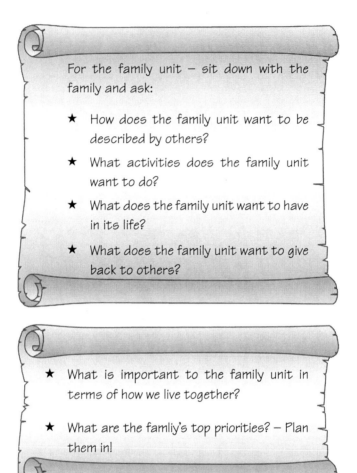

For the family unit – sit down with the family and ask:

★ How does the family unit want to be described by others?

★ What activities does the family unit want to do?

★ What does the family unit want to have in its life?

★ What does the family unit want to give back to others?

★ What is important to the family unit in terms of how we live together?

★ What are the famliy's top priorities? – Plan them in!

Ten days later...

Tom was out playing golf on Saturday morning. Unusually, PJ had phoned at the last minute to say that he couldn't make it, so Tom had decided to go anyway and have a round on his own. As he was walking up the ninth fairway a voice from the trees said, "So how did it go?"

Tom jumped back in surprise and muttered "Good grief," as The Magician appeared from behind the trees.

"Well there's lots going on. I want to know how it went. Did you have the meeting? How did it go? Are you going to take the new contract?"

As Tom continued his game he cast his mind back over the previous ten days and told The Magician all that had happened. The meeting with the team had been a great success. They'd closed the office for the day, and Suzie had answered the phones and taken messages. They held the meeting off-site at a local hotel. He'd been surprised at how productive the day had been and how keen the whole team were to get involved.

Zeb, one of the younger members of the team came up with some bizarre 'off the wall' ideas that Tom would never have considered. Andrea thought two or three had real potential so they'd spent time thinking them through and sure enough there were a couple of gems. And to Tom's delight they wouldn't cost a fortune to implement.

Together they'd worked out the business purpose. They'd also discussed what was important to them about how they worked together as a team. That had been a bit of an eye-opener Tom admitted to The Magician. He hadn't appreciated what a variety of perspectives there was in such a small group of people.

The outcome was that they'd agreed a team vision as well as quarterly and monthly goals so that everyone knew what was expected of them. Tom had agreed he would think about how he could link a performance bonus to the goals.

Finally it had been unanimously decided that they should take on the new business opportunity with Darren's firm. The best part of it was that the whole team were keen to do more and take on extra responsibility, so it looked as though they'd be able to handle it without the entire burden falling on Tom. That was good because Tom had already been through the same process with Suzie and she'd been against them taking on the contract if it meant that Tom would be spending a lot more time in the office.

The business would have to take on additional staff, but that was going to be less of an upheaval than Tom had expected. Carla had inducted Zeb and Chris – it was something Tom had delegated to her. But unbeknown to him she'd done rather more than he'd asked. In fact she'd written down the whole induction process, in a manual that everyone in the team could use to guide them through what to do when a new person joined. She said as she'd been learning the hard way, it seemed logical to write it all down so that she or someone else didn't need to 'reinvent the wheel' next time they recruited.

When The Magician heard what Carla had done he couldn't help smiling and saying to Tom "Isn't it great what people will do if you give them an opportunity and a little bit of support?"

"Yes," agreed Tom. "She's turning into a bit of a star."

"So it's all going well at work," said The Magician. "What about at home?"

"I went through the same process with the family. It was really Suzie and I, but we involved the kids as well. Katie surprised me. She said she wanted to spend some time alone with me. I hadn't thought about it, but she pointed out she gets time with Suzie after school twice a week before they collect the twins from nursery. Most of the time that she's with me the whole family is together. I had no idea that was what she wanted. So we're going to give it a try."

"That's great," said The Magician. "Those are just the sort of little things that never get addressed unless you put time aside for a proper discussion about what you want to achieve as a family and what's important to you as a family."

After a moment, he carried on "Now after all this positive news, is there anything that's concerning you?"

"Well yes there is one thing," said Tom. "But this next hole is a bit tricky, so can I concentrate on that for a minute."

"Of course," said The Magician. "Let me know when you're ready to talk again, I'm enjoying the walk and the fresh air."

If you would like to explore the concepts covered in this part of the story in more detail go to page 122 -133 and read Concepts 10, 11 & 12 or if you prefer, finish the story, and do the exercises at the end.

Chapter 5 – Time to let go...

A few minutes later ....

Tom was playing the last hole as he turned to The Magician and said, "My only concern now is how I'm going to keep it all going."

"You've come a long way in a short space of time," said The Magician. "Just think of all the work you've done developing yourself, your family and business relationships, not to mention all the work setting your direction for the future and the way you all work together. I think what you need to do now is think back to where you were before Christmas and write down all that's happened to get you where you are today. Then ask yourself what's missing?"

"What's missing?" repeated Tom vaguely as he concentrated on sinking his final putt. "What do you mean by that?" But of course it was too late. The Magician had already gone. There was a piece of paper tucked neatly inside Tom's golf trolley:

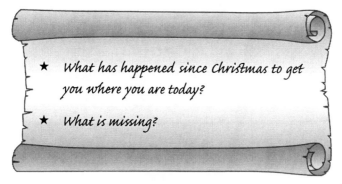

★ What has happened since Christmas to get you where you are today?

★ What is missing?

The following week…

In his office Tom was thinking about the things that had happened since Christmas. He got out all the pieces of paper that The Magician had given him and notes he had made from their conversations:

Using them as a prompt, Tom wrote out all the key points he could remember.

Getting Personal Balance:

- Where are you out of balance?

- How can you balance what you want with your ability to achieve what you want?

Setting Personal Purpose:

- What is important to you?

- How do you want to be described by others?

- What activities do you want to do?

- What do you want to have in your life?

- What do you want to give back to others?

Setting Business Purpose:

- How do you want the business to be described by others?

- What activities do you want the business to undertake?

- What do you want the business to have in terms of its assets?

- What do you want the business to give back to others?

- What's important to the team in terms of how they work together?

Setting Purpose for the family unit:

- How does the family unit want to be described by others?

- What activities do the family unit want to do?

- What does the family unit want to have in its life?

- What does the family unit want to give back to others?

- What's important to the family unit in terms of how we live together?

Based on how you would like things to be above:

- Identify three priorities (most important things) you would like to do in each particular area of your life – start with the areas of your life that are most important to you.

- Stick to the commitments which are important to you, and don't be distracted by urgent things which aren't as important.

- Listen to the people who you feel are important, talk, agree expectations, and understand what is important to them.

- Meet or manage the expectations of others.

- Look at all the tasks that you currently do and that need doing.

- Delegate tasks based on the ability and expectations of others.

- Think of anyone else who could help you achieve your objectives, whether they understand the task and what support they will need to do it. How long it will take to fully delegate responsibility to them?

- Start delegating!

- Involve the people who have a vested interest in the direction of the team in the development of the plan, and stretch their responsibilities, depending upon how they respond.

- Develop and refine team rules and values.

- Solve problems together.

He was amazed at how much he'd done over the months and the effect it had had on both his business and personal life. He could see how each task had built on the other tasks. It all looked so simple and logical now, he wouldn't dream of working any other way. All that was left was the final question 'what is missing?'

He said to himself "I don't think anything's missing."

"Are you sure?" said a quiet voice from behind him.

"Yes, I'm sure. I think we're done," he said absentmindedly.

Then he looked round with a start realising The Magician was actually in his office. "I thought I needed to be in the great outdoors, or at least out of the office, to find you."

"Well that just shows how relaxed you are, if you can find me whilst you're at your desk. What's all this about you thinking you're done? The point is you're never 'done' as you put it. That's what's missing. The only time anything is 'done' is when you close or sell the business. As long as it's running things will be moving and changing. You'll be constantly asking yourself, are you maintaining the balance?"

Whilst Tom was thinking that through, The Magician moved over to the desk where Tom had laid all the pieces of paper. They were in a long line and he moved the pieces so that they formed a circle with the first piece of paper resting with the last piece of paper to draw the circle together.

Then he said "You see you've put everything in place, but you've got to keep moving forward. The team are doing more, you're expecting more, but you still have to keep them motivated and you have to keep communicating, otherwise it could easily fall apart again."

"But that sounds even harder than the things I've done so far!" replied Tom looking worried.

"Well tell me, what support systems would you need to keep it in balance?" questioned The Magician.

"What do you mean by support systems?" enquired Tom.

"Things like training, coaching, rewards and recognition. How can you keep the team motivated and growing to get to the next stage? How will you evaluate what's happening so that you know what people need next? How will you communicate so that they feel involved in the process? How will you keep the team communicating as it grows? The way they resolve issues now is great, but how will you make sure that happens in the future?"

As Tom felt himself reeling under the weight of this list The Magician pressed on, "How are you going to continue developing the people and the business to deliver the results you're achieving now and more? We live in a constantly changing world Tom, and embracing change will allow you to move with it, keeping ahead of your competitors and the market."

With a twinkle he added, "Of course you need to keep an eye on your personal life and Suzie and the kids as well. Look at yourself; you're much healthier and happier than you were at Christmas. When was the last time your back pain niggled you?"

"It's so long ago I can't remember," said Tom looking blank.

"Well you must be doing something right." And with that The Magician was gone, leaving Tom pondering on support systems and change.

A clear November evening …

Tom was standing in the garden looking up at Orion wondering how he could make his peace with Suzie. Her brother Alexander had phoned the previous evening and announced that he was getting married the following Easter. Alexander had lived in New Zealand for over seven years and he'd met his fiancé over there. He wanted his Mum, Suzie and the family to go over for the wedding.

Of course Suzie had said they'd go, that wasn't the problem. It was the length of time she wanted to go for – four weeks! He'd told her point blank that he couldn't leave the business for more than ten days as it was at the moment. She'd said, "What's the point of running your own business if you can't get the freedom to leave now and again for a well earned break?" She felt that he was putting the business first again. It didn't help that she and her brother were still very close and spoke on the phone regularly, but whilst Alexander came back home occasionally, Suzie had never been to New Zealand.

As he was gazing at the stars he was aware of someone beside him. It wasn't Suzie.

"I hear you're going to New Zealand for four weeks," said The Magician.

"Well this time you heard wrong," snapped Tom. "I can't possibly go for more than a week, ten days at the most."

"Didn't you promise Suzie you would take two weeks off once Darren's contract was fully set-up and running smoothly?"

"Yes," replied Tom. "But I was only planning to go to Cornwall, or maybe France. Somewhere close enough that I could get back if there was a problem."

The Magician sighed, and then said, "Haven't you got a succession plan in place yet?"

"I'm not ready to die or retire yet you know," replied Tom.

"Succession plans aren't only for things like that, they're about preparing for the future and building in flexibility to deal with the unexpected – like a great opportunity to go to New Zealand. You know the world keeps changing and people will move on and new people will come in," said The Magician gently. "That goes for you too. Just because this is your business doesn't mean you have to manage it for life."

"I've never thought about doing anything else," said Tom.

"And maybe you'll never want to. But don't you think it would be sensible to have a plan in place in case you do. Look at Alexander, he only went to New Zealand for a holiday, but he loved it so much he decided to stay. And what about your key people? What if Andrea left? It would be pretty hard to replace her at the moment, wouldn't it?"

Tom didn't have to think long about that one. Andrea had been outstanding since they took on the new contract with Darren's firm. He would be lost without her.

Brightening a little he said, "I suppose a succession plan is also part of giving people opportunities to develop within the business. That way I'm less likely to lose key people like Andrea if she gets to the stage where she wants to do something new. And it fits with changes in direction by me or the business."

"Well," said The Magician. "A succession plan allows you to adapt. You can spend more time on business strategy when you get back from New Zealand, rather than working on the day-to-day stuff. You'll have given your team the opportunity to demonstrate their capability to run things without you."

The Magician continued, "Now, what you need to do is re-visit the business direction and objectives; think about the aspirations of key people and how they could grow within the business. You've mentioned Andrea so let's use her as an example," said The Magician. "There are a number of questions you will need to answer."

"What does Andrea want? If she takes on more responsibility how will you fill the gap she creates regarding her current responsibilities?" The Magician paused for effect. "What support does she need? And what affect does that have on the team and you?"

The Magician looked at Tom as the questions sank in. "Creating answers to these questions is the start of your succession plan Tom."

Tom looked at The Magician and nodded slowly, "I see what you mean now."

"Then," said The Magician. "You start the whole process off again with Andrea – get her to think about objectives, just like you did."

"So in many respects," said Tom. "We're starting again, going back to the beginning and thinking about direction, and objectives, but with other people taking more responsibility."

"Absolutely. It really completes the circle," said The Magician handing Tom another scroll.

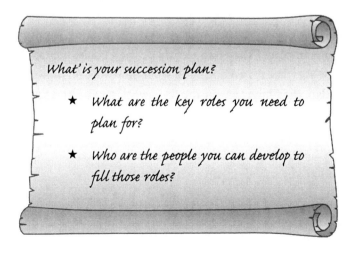

What is your succession plan?

★ What are the key roles you need to plan for?

★ Who are the people you can develop to fill those roles?

Christmas Eve…

He decided to go over to the sailing club before going home to the excitement of three children wanting to know when Santa would arrive!

As he sat on his familiar bench he looked back over the year. What a difference he thought to himself. A year ago he'd left the office on Christmas Eve not really expecting the business to survive the next few weeks. This year not only had he been to The Marlborough with the whole team, but he'd just announced a profit share because the business had done so well in the last six months.

This was one of the things he'd implemented in terms of support systems to keep the momentum going. He'd a whole host of other things to do before going to New Zealand at Easter, but the team were working well together. They'd agreed what needed doing to keep the business performing well and together they were putting support systems in place. They had clearly defined goals; they kept reviewing what they'd done and what they were planning to do. Also, they knew about the four-week trip he and Suzie were planning and had discussed it at one of their regular team meetings. He was coaching Andrea to take on his role whilst he was away and they were creating succession plans for other key roles, starting with hers.

He reflected on the last conversation he'd had with The Magician when they talked about succession plans. The Magician explained that Tom's role now was to guide others, just as The Magician had guided Tom. He was playing the conversation over in his mind, as if he was with The Magician now...

"It'll be your role Tom to guide Andrea just as I guided you. Your opportunity to pass on what you've learned – like leaving a legacy."

"So all this time, you've been getting me to this point, so that I can pass the same lessons on to others – to Andrea."

"Yes," said The Magician.

Tom continued, "And my role is to get Andrea to the point where she can pass these principles on to the rest of the team, to young Zeb perhaps."

"That's right," said The Magician. "But not only to Andrea, pass them on to all the people around you, to your work colleagues, friends, and your family. You are being a role model for them, demonstrating how things can be done."

Tom remembered The Magician looking at him squarely, and saying quietly, "For now, my work is done. It's over to you now Tom. If you need me, you know where to find me."

Tom became aware of the bench that he was sitting on and the view out to sea. He looked again at the final piece of paper and noticed the third question.

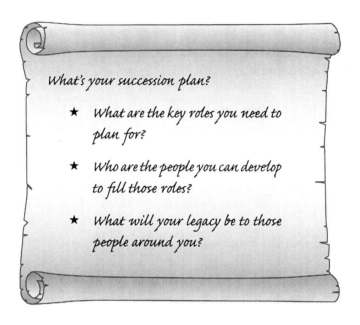

What's your succession plan?

★ *What are the key roles you need to plan for?*

★ *Who are the people you can develop to fill those roles?*

★ *What will your legacy be to those people around you?*

Tom thought about the business again and the fact that Andrea was looking forward to a new challenge. It was something she had been going to discuss at their next review meeting. Tom shook his head as he realised that only twelve months earlier he wouldn't have dreamt of spending time talking to people about what was important to them. Now he understood how valuable that really is.

He looked up as someone walked past. He'd half expected his Magician, but it was only a dog walker.

He hadn't seen The Magician since that night in November, and he wanted to tell him about the succession plans and how excited Suzie was about New Zealand. Then suddenly he realised, The Magician already knew. In fact he felt sure he'd be with him in New Zealand. Wherever he was, whatever he was doing, The Magician would always be there for him. All he had to do was make time for him, just like PJ's wise man.

As he looked out to sea, he said to himself, "Knowing what I know now, I wonder who else I could help find their inner Magician?"

He smiled as he realised things had come full circle. Now he was really looking forward to the future. He imagined what that would look, sound, and feel like: people developing with him, the business growing, more time with his family, feeling more relaxed about the business, knowing things were being done properly. He was actually enjoying thinking about the future.

Deep down, Tom recognised that he'd only just got to know The Magician and there was a lot more to learn from him. Tom had new questions he'd like answers to, but he also knew he needed to consolidate what he'd learned already and support others first.

He sensed that it wouldn't be too long before he had more things to discuss with The Magician... "But that will be a whole new chapter..." he said to himself as he got up and headed for his car.

If you would like to explore the concepts covered in this part of the story in more detail go to page 134 - 144 and read Concepts 13, 14 & 15 or if you prefer, finish the story, and do the exercises at the end.

Reflections on How to Lead Your Team... & Keep the Right Balance

In the following pages I will introduce you to The Leadership Matrix™. The principles built within it apply whether you lead a team of 1 (yourself) or 1000. Even though you might not be in a leadership position, The Leadership Matrix™ can still apply. Remember that leadership is a mindset not a position, if you interact with others in any way, then you are potentially leading them by your example. In this respect we are always leading someone.

In these reflections, I will briefly explore and discuss each principle that is shown in The Leadership Matrix™ (shown following). At the end of each group of concepts there is a note about how the concepts are illustrated in the story, as well as how you can use these to enhance your own leadership qualities.

The format for each concept explanation will be a summary of the principle involved, the objective of this concept from a leadership perspective, an explanation, and a key points summary.

The first three concepts are all about setting the scene, or to put it another way 'the big picture stuff'. This is essential to move forward effectively. They are shown in the highlighted circle at the centre of the diagram.

The Leadership Matrix™

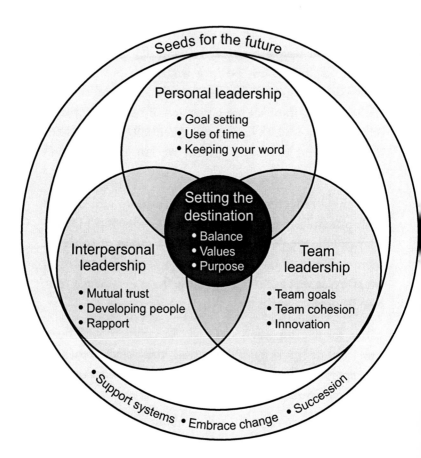

Setting the destination - Where are you heading?

Setting the destination forms the foundation for all the other aspects of leadership within the Leadership Matrix. By setting the destination you form the context within which all the other sections will work. Setting the destination comprises of your purpose and your values which will form the guidance system of how you will operate, and maintaining a balance between the results you achieve and your ability to produce those results.

Without a clear idea of your purpose, and your values, decisions about your goals and use of time become more difficult. Without maintaining balance, it becomes increasingly difficult to sustain results in the long term. Setting the direction then, forms the core of the Leadership Matrix, and so rightly fits within the inner centre circle of the diagram

Concept 1 - Balance - Performance vs capacity

Principle

To make sure that you or your team perform well, you will need to do the things necessary to develop your ability to perform well.

Objective

To maintain the ability of you and your team to perform at a consistently high level, and sustain the results that you want.

Explanation

Balance is fundamental to your success in any role in life. To create balance you need to have a view of the whole picture and have all the smaller aspects that make up the whole, working in harmony together. In terms of leadership, balance is about knowing what objective you want to achieve and understanding how you can set up all of your resources and circumstances to impact on your ability to achieve your objective. This includes not only all the aspects of the business, but of your personal life to. To use an example, it is easy to put every ounce of effort into one area of your life to get a short-term result, but if you keep focussing on that area to the neglect of other aspects of your life, in the long-term, your ability to get results will diminish.

In simple terms the kind of balance we are talking about here is balancing the activities which you do to get the results you want, with the things you could do to improve or increase your abilities to get results. If you continually push for results, at the expense of developing or maintaining ability, the results will eventually diminish.

To get good performance from a car for example, you need to maintain its working parts, if you don't maintain the car, it will eventually let you down. This is a good metaphor for life. Maintenance is just as important as results.

These days there is a lot of talk about work/life balance. To keep achieving, it is recognised that no one can work hard all the time - you need rest and relaxation. You need a balance between the time and effort you spend at work and the time and effort you spend on the rest of your life, otherwise you will 'burn out'.

In the context of leadership, to keep in balance you need to establish what to do personally to ensure you are always able to maintain your optimum performance as a leader. Having established what that is, it is your responsibility to make time to balance the results that you get with your ability to produce those results.

The same applies to the teams, people, or systems, which you lead. The fact is that when you are in a leadership position others will follow your example. Since you will no doubt be responsible for the results of the people you lead, it is vital that they understand the importance of both 'maintenance' and 'results'. They will gain that understanding by observing what you do, and the example you set.

At an individual level, 'maintenance' activities are very personal; one person's way to maintain their ability, is another person's stress that could diminish ability, so allow people to identify their own way. In this respect, our own 'magician' can guide us to what is right and wrong for us. Pay attention to the signals, and you will soon identify which activities 'maintain' you and which activities get results.

Key points:

- Identify the key things that you need to do to sustain your ability to perform well.

- Devote time to those things.

- Check regularly to ensure that the things you are doing are working.

- Remember that different people react to different forms of support and maintenance.

Concept 2 - Values - What's important to you?

Principle

To lead in the way that you would like to, so that you can be a role model, you will need to be clear in your own mind what is important to you, and how you lead.

Objective

Having clarity of your values, so that when you need to make an important decision about direction, you can do so based on a core foundation of what is important – what is 'right' or 'wrong' for you or your team.

Explanation

Values are those things, which are most important to you. Throughout your life you will be motivated to meet your values, even though you may not be totally aware of what they are. The reason they are called values is because they are powerful motivators in the way you run your life. They are quite simply those things that have value to you. Often they can be quite abstract, and they are highly personal. Two people could have the same words for their values, and yet have quite a different meaning for those words. Being successful may be a value, but how do you describe success? Your description will almost certainly be different from someone else's description of success.

Work values are the things that are most important to you in terms of your work. Life values are the things that are most important to you in terms of your life in general. If you change the context, then your values may change. For example what is important about the car you drive, what is important about the friends you have, what is important to you about the books you read. These different contexts will highlight different values.

Remember that values are personal to you. Your own values will tend to be subjective. Other people will have different values. They are such an intrinsic part of who you are, that often you may not notice them. You may assume those things are equally important to everyone else. Often that is not the case, which is why you may find it hard to understand how other people can behave in ways that are unimaginable to you.

Once you are aware of your own values you can use them more consciously as a guidance system for decisions that you make. Knowing your values will allow you to consider whether a particular path will take you closer to or further away from your values, which may make the decision process very much easier for you.

In the context of leadership, your values will act like a guide, ensuring that the decisions you make are more likely to be in alignment with your values. When leading a team, if the team have identified their values, then they can make decisions more easily.

The clarity you will have, allows you as the team leader to justify decisions which are aligned with your values, and reject decisions which are misaligned with your values.

Key points:

- Take time to identify what is important to you within various contexts, and particularly in the context in which you lead. (See the list of questions The Magician asked Tom)

- Review your values regularly they can change over time.

- If you are about to make an important decision, consult your values.

- The bulk of your motivation will relate to your core values. The likelihood is that you will be motivated to do something which is aligned with your values, and not motivated about something which is misaligned with your values.

Concept 3 - Purpose - What are you about?

Principle

If you have clarity of your purpose, you are more likely to devote time and resources to do things, which are aligned with your purpose.

Objective

To make sure that you know your purpose so that you can use it as the basis for the decisions you make.

Explanation

Your values will combine with your overall purpose or direction to provide the canvas or backdrop for all your decisions. As a leader you need a clear purpose to focus and guide your own actions and to motivate your team.

Answering the following questions is a very simple, yet effective way of working out your overall purpose:

- How do you want to be described by others?

- What activities do you want to do?

- What do you want to have in your life?

- What do you want to give back to others?

- What is important to you?

These questions are repeated again in the 'Your Task' section at the end of this chapter.

Let's use a simple exercise, to help you decide how you want to be described by others. Imagine you are at an 80th birthday celebration - your own 80th birthday. People are gathered together to describe you and how they see you. How would you like them to describe you and your life, or what you mean to them? What would you want them to say? Whatever answers you come up with to those questions, will help you identify the answers you need.

What you want to do refers to tasks, actions and activities that will fill your life. Explore what you want to do as a job or career, hobby or interest, places to visit, people to be with, and so on. It might help you to consider what you really love doing, or what you dream of doing in the future.

The things you have in your life, are what you own, these can be both tangible and intangible. To achieve certain goals you may need to acquire particular assets. They are not always monetary, for example you may want to have the 'asset' of friendship. Think about what you want to have in relation to all areas of your life.

We live in a world where everyone and everything is interdependent. What you want to give back asks how you provide support or service in many different forms. In a business context it may be the benefit you bring to a customer or employee. In a personal context it may be the joy you bring to your family. In a social context it may be the support you give to a local charity or the mentoring you provide for young people.

Gaining clarity in your 'purpose' will, like values, allow you to make decisions and choices based on a longer-term overall strategy, rather than what seems popular today.

Think of values and purpose as acting like a compass bearing. No matter what life throws at you, you will have a reference point to refer back to. You can then make decisions based on whether a choice will take you closer to or further from the values and purpose you have identified.

Key Points:

- Gain clarity on your purpose or intention. This can be balanced across different parts of your life, maybe personal, family, or career.

- Before you agree to an activity ask 'what is my intention here?'

- Check if an activity or decision is taking you closer to or further from your purpose for that part of your life.

How Tom explores balance, values & purpose

In the first chapter Tom is challenged to consider every aspect of his life and the extent to which it impacts on his current situation. This forces him to see how much he doesn't know and how much he has lost awareness of the things that are most important to him. This realisation is an important starting point giving him the impetus to begin from fundamental principles.

The questions Tom is invited to consider address his balance, values and purpose. Although he is confused at first, as he explores his values and purpose, he realises how interconnected they are, and he begins to see value in the time he devotes to clarifying them, as they will form the basis of his future decisions.

Your task

Answer these questions for your yourself:

- What is important to you? What else is important? (make a list). You can rank the importance if you want to, from most to least important.

- Is your life in balance? Or to put it another way, are you addressing the areas of your life that are important to you in a balanced way?

- How do you want to be described by others?

- What activities do you want to do?

- What do you want to have in your life?

- What do you want to give back to others?

You can answer these questions in any order that works for you. You may find that as you think about one, answers to another will also come into focus. The important thing is to relax, not be interrupted and give yourself as much time as you need. Tackling these questions is the foundation of the leadership process.

The Leadership Matrix™

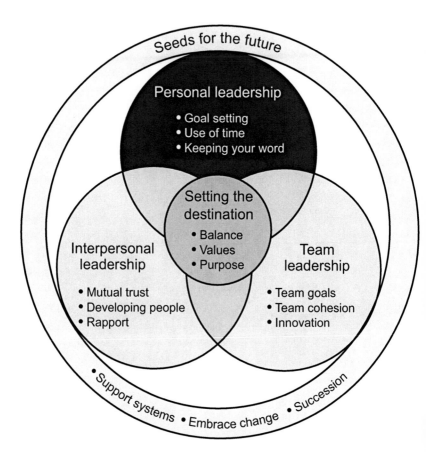

Personal leadership - Organising Yourself

Personal leadership relates to how you organise yourself so that people know what to expect of you, and perhaps more importantly, they know that they can trust you to do what you say you will do. The aspects of Personal Leadership are shown in the circle at the top of The Leadership Matrix™.

Concept 4 - Goal setting - Milestones of progress

Principle

To make your purpose real and have practical meaning it will need to be broken down into bite-sized-pieces. Goal setting is the process that is used to convert aspirations into goals that are 'SMART'. That is specific, measurable, achievable, relevant, and time related.

Objective

To be able to translate your purpose, or vision of the future into measurable steps or actions, so that everyone involved, can understand their contribution to your purpose.

Explanation

Values (Concept 2) and purpose (Concept 3) are all about deciding on the big picture. Goal setting is about translating something as abstract and visionary as a purpose into manageable sized pieces that will help you to get from where you are today, to where you want to be.

For a purpose to be achieved it will be necessary to break it down into action points, only then does it become a goal. Up until that point, arguably it is just an aspiration.

For example if one of your values is good health, you might want to set some goals for how often you go to the gym, or how far you run or walk each day. You might make these goals progressive, saying you want to swim three times a week for 20 minutes this month and increase that to five times a week for 40 minutes next month and so on. The aspiration of good health is obtained by achieving the goals set in the form of exercise targets.

The key aspect here is not only identifying the long-term goal, but also identifying the steps that make up the goal, and to plan them into a diary or system for making them happen. The next section on use of time will look at this in more detail.

Key points:

Things to consider when setting goals are as follows:

- The level of desire to achieve the goal, and the benefits of achieving it.

- Whether the goal helps you achieve your purpose.

- Things that could get in the way of achieving the goal.

- Resources necessary.

- Tasks to be completed.

- People involved, and which tasks they will do or could help with.

- How the tasks will be communicated to those people.

- How completion of tasks and the goal will be measured.

- How you will celebrate achievement of the tasks and the goal.

Concept 5 - Use of time - Balance in practice

Principle

The way you use time sends a signal to those you lead. Use your time to move closer to your purpose, values, and objectives, doing anything less than this is wasting time and encourages others to do the same.

Objective

To choose to allocate time to those activities which take you closer to your goals or purpose, and to allocate little or no time to activities, which do not add value to you.

Explanation

How you manage your time is critical when you are a leader. There is generally a lot to do and there are often unexpected crises to demand your time when you planned to be doing something else. The values, purpose, and goals that you identified earlier, will allow you to make clear decisions regarding how you use your time.

The way that you use your time has a big influence on whether or not you feel in balance. If you give time to something, which is not important to you, and therefore potentially give less time to something that is more important to you, you will probably feel out of balance.

It may seem so ridiculous to even be tempted to do something that is against your values and purpose. In reality people often do just that, especially, if the less important task is easier to tackle, or is more familiar. People often do things that they like to do, or are more popular, ahead of doing things which they should be doing, but which may be more difficult to do.

People often mix up urgency and importance, causing them to do things, which are urgent, rather than those things which are genuinely important. Remember that urgent and important are not the same thing. Things that are important usually have consequences that will move you towards your purpose. Things that are urgent are related to time and usually have a deadline attached. These same deadlines can often be artificial, normally imposed by someone else who is simply working to a timetable, without necessarily adding real value.

Something that is both urgent and important should take top priority. Something that is urgent but not important should actually have a very low priority and a good leader will question whether it is worth doing at all.

Let me give you an example to illustrate this point. In many organisations, people complete forms and prepare reports because it is part of their job. It is something on the list of things to do which has always been there.

For the purpose of illustration we will use the story of Alan. Alan was asked to create a report for his boss, which summarised all of the sales for a region. The report was produced by the fourth day of every month. A change in circumstances meant that his boss would need the information a day earlier, and he obtained it verbally. Alan then produced the report which he had always produced so that his boss had confirmation…after the meeting for which his boss needed the information!

Why did he do this? He did it because it was on his list of things to do each month. Alan's boss never stopped him producing the report, just in case he needed the confirmation. In twelve months of completing this report, how many times did Alan's boss actually need the written report? NONE!

Now, does this happen in real life? Absolutely, in my years as a consultant I've seen example after example of this happening. A person doing a task, without really understanding why they are doing it. They don't see how it fits into the bigger picture, because they don't know the bigger picture. The real shame is that a person doing a task like this, is being prevented from doing something that truly adds value.

So the best question to ask is whether doing the task is going to take you closer to your purpose or objective, and is it genuinely more important than what you currently have planned? By doing this you will start to focus your time on the things that matter to you. This does of course presuppose that you have identified your purpose and values. Many people haven't, which again explains why they do tasks that are not adding value.

A point worthy of note here is that you may sometimes choose to complete a task which seems to take you away from your purpose. You do it because it's for a person who is important to you. It's the relationship which is important, not the task. Logically then, you could still complete the task and feel good about it, because you are supporting a relationship which you value.

Key points:

- Identify your values and purpose for the role in question, as highlighted in the earlier concepts. This forms the basis for good use of time.

- Identify whether a task is important by checking if it will take you closer to or further away from your intended purpose.

- Then, separately ask how urgent is the task in relation to its deadline.

Concept 6 - Keeping your word - keeping promises to yourself and others

Principle

The actions you take in relation to the promises you make, will determine the extent to which people will trust you in the long-term. A leader who is not trusted by the people arund him will simply not be able to get help when he needs it. Many of the symptoms of leaders in difficulty can be traced to a lack of trust. More will be covered on this subject in concept 7.

Objective

To engender loyalty and trust from the people around you, by consistently keeping to your word, and demonstrating your trustworthiness.

Explanation

Keeping your word is a major aspect of personal leadership. There is a strong expectation from others that you will do what you say. Keeping your commitments on a regular basis demonstrates your personal integrity, and here it is definitely a case of actions speaking louder than words.

It is relatively easy to decide how to use your time and to set yourself goals for the short and medium term. The hard bit is actually making it happen!

If you do what you say you will do, you begin to live your values and the people in your life will notice. They will see that you are a person of your word, and that you keep your promises, and this in turn creates trust.

When you demonstrate the principles of personal leadership, you are being a role model for people around you and demonstrating your trustworthiness.

People will begin to listen to you, and follow you out of choice. You are being a role model for them to follow, particularly if you are demonstrating the behaviours which they value, thus implying similar values.

You might have seen the opposite of this in real life. For example, where a business or a leader sets a vision and values amidst a great fanfare about how this is a new step for the future, but the following day all the decisions are taken exactly as they were before. This is when people become sceptical and stop taking notice of what they are being told. In effect they stop trusting their leadership.

Keeping your word is the foundation for developing trust (Concept 7) so it is important that you focus on how you can bring integrity to everything you do. For now, you need to focus on your task - this is your chance to keep a commitment to yourself!

Key Points:

- Be careful what you commit to. Before you make a commitment, be sure that you have a reasonable chance of keeping it.

- Once you have made a commitment, do everything you can to keep it, or have a very clear explanation why you can't.

How Tom explores use of time, goal setting and keeping his word

When Tom has an urgent issue at work that means he cancels his dinner date with Suzie the repercussions are rather more than he expected. This all happens in Chapter 2 and it gives Tom several lessons not only in the use of his time, but also setting goals for the things that matter to him, as well as keeping his word.

By focusing on these three aspects of his personal behaviour Tom will enhance his qualities as a leader as he acts with integrity and is seen as more trustworthy. This is vital as a foundation for developing trust with others, as you will see in the next concept.

Your task

- Go back to your answers to the questions at the end of Chapter 1; these will be the foundation for your values and purpose.

- Take the list of values, and put them in order from most to least important.

- Ask yourself if you are devoting a balanced amount of time to the top three?

- Ask yourself what you mean by each value, and create a description for each value, and how it would be, or what you would be doing to meet that value.

- Identify three goals or tasks, which you could plan into your diary to meet the top three values you have identified.

- To help you plan the goals properly, use the following checklist for each of the three goals identified:

  - Does achieving this goal take you closer to your purpose?

  - What could get in the way of you achieving this goal?

  - What resources do you need?

  - What tasks need to be completed to achieve the goal?

  - Who could help you and how?

  - How will you measure completion?

  - How will you celebrate completion?

- Create your plan based on the answers to the above questions, and then follow your plan.

When another opportunity crops up to distract you from your short term goal or long term purpose, (and it no doubt will) make your choice based on what is genuinely more important not just urgent.

The Leadership Matrix™

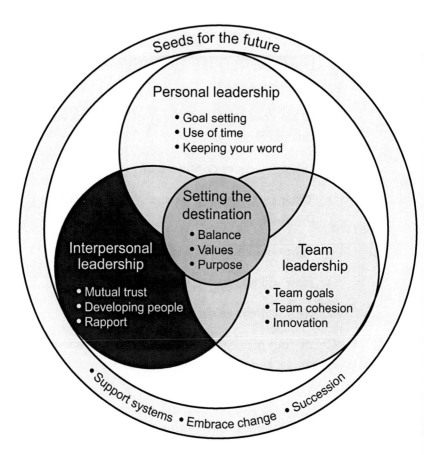

Interpersonal leadership - Developing your relationship with others

Interpersonal leadership is about the way that you interact with other individuals in your role as leader. The next three concepts will help you to excel in this. They are shown in the bottom left circle of The Leadership Matrix™.

In todays world we are interdependent upon each other to get things done. Even if you don't lead anyone formally, it is in your interests to build trusting relationships with others so that they are willing to support you when you need it.

As highlighted earlier, Personal Leadership forms the foundation for Interpersonal Leadership. If your Interpersonal Leadership is not going well, then check first that you have put the right foundations in place by carrying out the steps of Personal Leadership.

Concept 7 – Mutual trust

Principle

Trust is two-way, and will grow or deplete depending upon how people are treated. One trustworthy person in a relationship is not enough, for trust to really thrive both parties must be trustworthy in each other's eyes.

Objective

To develop a relationship of mutual trust, where both

parties keep to their word and look after the interests of each other.

Explanation

Trust takes time to develop and it is difficult to define; yet it is a vital component of any on-going relationship. Once people see you consistently keep your commitments they will begin to trust you.

In his book 'The 7 Habits of Highly Effective People', Stephen Covey describes trust within all types of relationship as being rather like a bank account. When you do things which are in line with or better than people's expectations, your action puts a deposit in their account. On the other hand if you fail to meet someone's expectations, it is like a withdrawal from their account.

The more withdrawals you make, potentially the more overdrawn an account becomes. In my experience this usually shows itself in cynicism towards you or your actions. Conversely if you have put in many deposits over time, then people will have more faith in you, and when you make a withdrawal if it is a genuine mistake, they will be more tolerant. A deliberate withdrawal is however, different, and can have a massive negative effect on the account.

The key aspect to bear in mind with this concept is that withdrawals and deposits are based on the perception of the person holding the account, and have little or no objectivity. They are purely subjective.

To illustrate this point let me give you an example:

Imagine that one of your colleagues pays you a compliment about the way that you look. How do you translate the meaning of their interaction? Was the interaction positive or negative? Did they mean it, or were they after something? Were they being sarcastic? It depends on your perception and what you regard as 'normal' for that person.

The key to developing trust is the level of consistency in your actions. If for whatever reason the bank account of trust is overdrawn, it may take consistent deposits, to clear a negative account. While the account is clearing, despite the deposits, which you are making, the person may seem just as 'cynical' or 'negative' as they were from the beginning. When sufficient deposits have been made the relationship should improve. In most instances your persistence will pay off, and the relationship will be stronger for it.

The type of withdrawals and deposits will have a different impact on the relationship depending upon the person, their perception of you, and the circumstances. Withdrawals and deposits that have the highest impact both negatively and positively are usually aligned with a person's values for 'relationship'. If you cross a person's value for 'relationship' it will have a dramatic affect.

So, if for example one of your values for 'relationship' is being on time, and one of your colleagues continually arrives late when you meet, this would have a very detrimental affect on your relationship. Another person faced with the same situation however may not be affected, if 'being on time' is not one of their values. This illustrates how relationships can become strained when the simplest things are interpreted in different ways. Often it is simply down to expectations not being discussed and agreed.

Key points:

- Ask the people around you what their expectations are for your relationship.

- Explain to them your expectations, and come to an agreement.

- In your interactions with other people, ensure that you meet their expectations or explain why you can't.

- If someone is not meeting your expectations after you have agreed them, raise your concerns and agree a satisfactory solution.

Concept 8 - Developing people - engaging people and helping them grow

Principle

To achieve your purpose you will probably need the help of others. In my experience people are generally willing to help you if you make it a positive experience, so it makes sense for you to help them to develop their capability to to help you. Expecting a person to perform well in a changing environment without development and support is like expecting a plant to grow without food or water.

Objective

To identify the skills and capabilities you need in the people around you in order to deliver your purpose and objectives. Then engage people with those skills and capabilities to help you.

Explanation

Developing people links strongly to the concept of Balance (Concept 1). 'Balance' means you need to make sure that the results you want are balanced with your ability to get those results. In a business context this means that as a business grows you will need more people, or greater capability. Your people will need to produce or do more, to keep achieving the results that you want to achieve.

If you are following the principles of Personal Leadership you will be keeping your word and as a result you will develop trust as shown above. Once you have developed trusting relationships with the individual members of your team they will probably want to do more to help you achieve your goals.

Once you have the foundation of trust you can create opportunities for people to do more, or to do different things. In this way you will build sustainability as your team grows. Before giving someone a new opportunity you need to consider if they have the necessary knowledge, skills and attitude to do what you want them to do. The right attitude is the most important thing as knowledge and skills can usually be acquired through training or coaching. The right attitude is usually intrinsic, it's either there or it's not. My suggestion is that you engage people based on attitude first, knowledge and skills second.

When you are giving people new opportunities remember that they may need extra support along the way. Sometimes they will make mistakes, it is important then to remain supportive and look at the lessons learned for the future, rather than starting to blame the individual. Remember the person will be doing the best that they can with the knowledge, skills and attitude that they have at the time. Allowing them to grow and develop means that they do things whilst they are learning new skills or acquiring new knowledge.

One of the greatest motivators for staff is positive feedback and development; it engenders great loyalty, because they see that you are investing in them. Equally one of the biggest reasons for people to start looking to leave one team for another is lack of praise and development. Look for every opportunity to give praise and feedback.

Recognise something that the person has done well for you, and highlight how they could do something more effectively. A word of caution though, as covered before, if trust is low they may be cynical to this at first.

Key points:

- Identify the skills and capabilities you need to have available to deliver your objectives and purpose.

- Evaluate the skills and capabilities you have within your team members now.

- Create a plan to bridge the gap between the two, and involve others in the creation of the plan. By default you will have to also involve them in understanding your purpose, values, and objectives, this will help them understand the contribution they can make.

Concept 9 - Rapport - 'Getting on' with people

Principle

People like people like themselves, even if it is only a perceived likeness. If you have rapport with people, they are more likely to follow you. You can adapt your style of interaction to generate rapport.

Objective

To gain rapport with people, so that communication is open, honest, multi-directional, and supportive.

Explanation

Rapport occurs when two people communicate really easily together. It is easiest to develop rapport with people who have similar values to you. It is harder to develop rapport with people who have very different values, unless you are open to understanding people with different values and outlooks and tend to celebrate those differences.

The first stage in developing true rapport is to understand the other person's values. But remember values are so intrinsic to each of us that you and the other person may think they are obvious, so you both need to share your values openly and honestly to ensure they are properly understood. They are unlikely to match exactly, by sharing them you will see the similarities and differences.

Understanding another person's values and openly respecting differences between you will develop trust and respect as well as rapport.

Much has been written about the technique of rapport. Any good book on Neuro Linguistic Programming, will provide you with a great deal of highly detailed information on generating rapport. When people are in rapport their non-verbal communication is very similar, so one of the ways to initiate rapport is to mirror a person's body language.

There are a number of things you can mirror:

- Their posture

- The tone of their voice

- The words they use

Another major aspect of rapport is to truly listen to people. Show that you are listening by regularly summarising what they have said to check your understanding.

Key points:
- Generate rapport with people by listening to them, asking questions, and being genuinely interested in what they have to say.

- Show that you are listening by summarising your understanding of what they have said, and how they said it.

- Be flexible in the way you interact and make people at ease by being like them.

How Tom explores developing mutual trust, developing people and rapport

In Chapter 3 Tom learns about how to be effective in one-to-one relationships with other members of his team. As he finds that he cannot do everything himself he sees how his personal leadership skills impact on the relationships that he has with members of his team.

As he keeps his word, and uses time effectively so he shows his trustworthiness, and until he is seen as trustworthy he cannot develop trust with other people. Once he develops trust and rapport with each person in his business, it is easier for him to develop that person, and delegate tasks to them.

Your task

Consider the relationships that you have with others. Pick your two closest relationships first and think:

- What are the other person's expectations of me?

- What would they think are withdrawals in our relationship?

- What would they think are deposits in our relationship?

Then have a conversation with the person involved and ask them what is important to them about how you support your relationship and interact with them.

Consider which of your goals could be supported by someone else.

- Who could support you?

- Will they want to do it?

- Is your relationship ready for you to ask for support?

- What support do they need in order to support you?

- How long will it take to fully complete this task?

Have a conversation and really try to understand the other person and their situation. Regularly summarize what they have said and how you think they feel.

The Leadership Matrix™

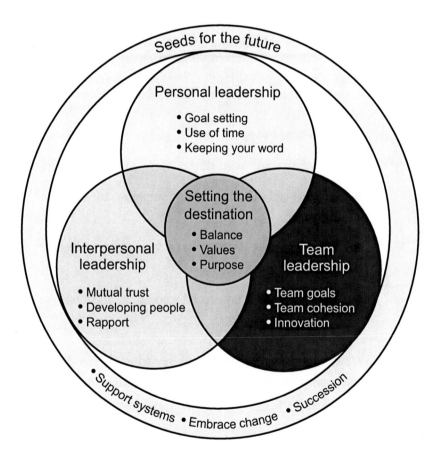

Team leadership - Getting the team members to support each other

A quick word on teams. When I refer to 'the team', this may be a formal team of the kind you would find in a business, or an informal team for example within a social group. In this way a team is just a group of individuals who share a vision or common aim communicated by a leader, however that vision has come about.

Team leadership is what makes a leader most visible to the outside world. The concepts that help you to achieve this are shown in the bottom right circle of The Leadership Matrix™.

The effect of getting a team to work well together is almost magical, and yet the foundations identified in Chapters 1 to 3 must be in place in order for the team results to be sustainable. Without the foundations of trust, and a clear purpose a strong team is just not possible. Equally a strong team is made up of strong individuals, so people will need to be engaged at an individual level, before the team can work at its best.

Concept 10 - Team goals - Involving the team in their future

Principle

Involve people in setting objectives, and finding ways of achieving them, they will probably find better and more effective ways than you would have thought of.

Objective

To set team goals in a way that engenders ownership by the team, and encourages them to find their own way of achieving the goals.

Explanation

Leaders tend to think strategically, whilst team members usually operate tactically. The challenge for the leader is to provide the link between the big picture vision and the detail level operations that are needed to achieve the vision. Involving the team in this process of translating vision to detailed goals is the key.

To me the phrase 'without involvement there is no commitment' epitomises the concept of team goals. For the team to work well together and support you as a leader they need to be involved in setting their own targets and deciding how they work together to help the team achieve its ultimate ambitions.

If the team are truly a part of the process and can see that their input has been valued they will be far more committed to the goals that are set as a team, for the team. Also because you are using input from several people you will often develop innovative ideas and suggestions – for more about innovation see Concept 12.

Some poor leaders abuse the process of developing team goals by asking the team to take part in the process, but without taking any real notice of their thoughts and suggestions. The end result is what the leader wanted regardless of whether it is practical or whether the team feel any ownership of it. This type of approach will lose the trust and support of the team, as they will perceive that the behaviour lacks integrity.

In order for the team to take ownership of the objective, they must trust you and your intentions. If you are struggling to get people to take ownership, it may well be a symptom of a lack of trust. The basis of this is the trustworthiness of you and your leadership, so go back to the section on Personal Leadership to review the main points.

When the team fully understand their goals, they will understand the expectations you have of them, and often will progress towards the goal with very little supervision or checking. They understand the goal, and want to succeed, and when these are in place you simply need to get out of the way and let them get on with it.

Key points:

- Involve people in setting their own goals.

- Show a clear link between the team goals, individual goals and the overall purpose.

- Encourage people to create their own way of doing things, they will probably be better than your way.

Concept 11 - Team cohesion - Agreed values - the glue which holds the team together

Principle

When there is high trust within a team, very little supervision is needed, they solve their own problems, and come up with better ideas as a team than any one individual could realise. There is a level of synergy within the team that generates results, which far surpass expectations again and again.

Objective

To create an atmosphere within the team of mutual trust and respect. Each team member can then thrive, offer suggestions, and make mistakes without fear of recriminations from you or his colleagues.

Explanation

When I explained about developing mutual trust in Concept 7, the focus was on developing trust between individual people. Team cohesion is about developing that trust and understanding not just between individuals but also across a whole team.

Each team member will have expectations of the team and the other team members, which is fine as long as everyone knows what the expectations are. Taking the time to identify those expectations and agree the rules within which you will work together, will help develop team cohesion. Without doing that there is a risk that each person will act according to their own expectations and values on the assumption that all other people are the same – which of course they are not!

Symptoms which you see in ineffective teams include people blaming others, moaning, complaining, one-upmanship and petty quarrels. Clarifying the rules sets up the basis for the team to work well together and resolve any conflict quickly.

Agreeing team rules is quite simple. It is the same process that you used to discover your values in Concept 2. You bring the team together and ask each person 'what's important to you about how we work together?' It takes careful facilitation, and can sometimes get a bit heated – after all people are passionate about their values. As long as you control the process well, the results can be enormously empowering. In terms of the practicalities allow each team member to speak in turn, using a dice or something similar to decide the order that people speak. Ensure that the other team members do not make any judgements; questions can be asked if they need clarification.

After that ask the team to collectively agree their combined values or rules of engagement. Notice that people can use different words and mean the same thing, so you need to ask, 'what do you mean by... (value)...' and get them to describe it. Then you can look for overlaps in meaning with other people's values, you will often be surprised at how similar they are!

Taking the time to help the team agree their rules of engagement can have a far reaching and powerful effect within the team. The reason for this is that a foundation of trust with the leader is already in place. Remember to take whatever time it takes to get this right, in the long run it will probably be one of the most worthwhile things you ever did with your team.

Key points:

- The same principles which apply to trust between you and your team, also apply between team members.

- Help the team members identify their expectations of each other, and of you, so that you can agree a set of team rules or norms.

- Help team members understand the concept of trust, and the effect that meeting or not meeting expectations can have on trust and the relationship.

The process outlined could be used just as effectively before the team completes a one-off task, as it could be for a team which will stay together for a long time. By agreeing expectations early, you will enhance results and potentially save time otherwise spent resolving petty disputes.

Concept 12 - Innovation - Synergy, when 1+1>2 - the art of celebrating difference

Principle

When people who have a mutually agreed aim come together in an environment of mutual support and respect, they can work together to create solutions, which would never have been possible had they tried to identify them on their own. Yet when they work together, the development of ideas can be almost effortless.

Objective

To create an environment where team members value each other's contribution, and will work together to find better solutions than any one individual team member could have created.

Explanation

Innovation is defined in the Chambers Concise Dictionary as 'introducing something new'. In terms of your role as a leader it is likely to be about new ways of working. Within teams, most innovative ideas come about when the team are working well together so that you get what is known as synergy.

Synergy occurs when you generate better results from combining elements to work together, than you would have achieved by having those elements working separately. You have probably experienced the effect when you have been generating ideas with friends or solving a problem. You may have struggled to create a solution to a problem on your own. When you work with others on the same problem, one person comes up with the start of a solution that the next person builds upon, and then another person builds on that. This carries on to the point where the combination of all the suggestions together is better than any one member of the team could have devised.

Using teams to find innovative ways of working is a good thing to do when you are faced with a challenge that means that the old way of doing things is no longer effective. For example, if a customer needs you to halve your price, or if a competitor has a new process that means they are working twice as fast, your old ways of working will not be effective. In these situations, to remain competitive you need to find ways to innovate.

It is just these kinds of challenging situations, which force us to think creatively to solve problems which we otherwise would not have faced.

Often it is difficult for people who know the process well to look at it from an innovative viewpoint. One option is to bring in some people who know little about the process. They can stimulate the discussion with new ideas, which people with in-depth knowledge and understanding can then build into a workable solution.

The key to the whole process is a feeling of safety and mutual trust. If team members feel it is ok to make suggestions which will not be 'judged', then they will do so. What starts as a radical idea can become a ground-breaking reality, when it is translated by a strong team, which celebrates each other's contribution.

Throughout history this has been the case, so why not help your team make history?

What ideas could they come up with given the right environment and support?

Key points:

- Encourage people to suggest new ideas, and ensure that they are all valued. An average suggestion can quickly develop into an outstanding idea when people discuss and contribute to it.

- Don't dismiss anything in the early stages; let the team kick ideas around.

- Embrace challenges as opportunities to 'break the old rules' to see what you can come up with.

- Follow through with rigorous action plans to convert ideas into reality.

How Tom explores team goals, team cohesion and innovation

In Chapter 4 Tom gets to the point where he can involve his team in the purpose of the business and the delivery of his objectives. Tom also discovers that when the team have agreed what is important, they understand the priority of the tasks, and it makes delegation much easier.

Tom also uses the team to explore how they can adapt to meet the needs of the new business opportunity. The whole team together generates ideas that Tom would not have thought of on his own, giving Tom valuable lessons in how to generate innovative ideas in the future.

Your task

- Identify your 'team' whether that is a work team or your family unit or partner, or a social or informal group.

- Ask the team what they want collectively in terms of:

o Being described by others?

o Activities they want to do?

o What they want to have as a team?

o What they want to give back to others as a team?

- Ask each member in turn, what is important about how they work together. This can be completed as a group as long as each person is allowed to give their answers without interruption.

- Ask the team to decide the goals that will be the stepping-stones to get to the purpose that you have agreed. Remember the goals need to be in line with the team's values too.

- Once you have involved the team in agreeing their future vision and rules of engagement, put it into practice, and review it regularly to make sure that you and the team are on track.

- Celebrate and encourage new ideas.

The Leadership Matrix™

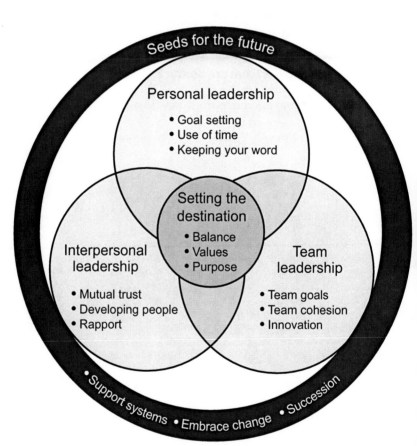

Seeds for the future - creating a legacy

These last three concepts are about how to maintain momentum and keep everything in balance as things change around you. The outer circle of The Leadership Matrix™ shows these as they provide the boundary that protects and maintains everything else.

Concept 13 - Support systems - maintaining the momentum you have created so far

Principle

Appropriate support systems ensure that the team can keep achieving the results which you have set, without being distracted. Support systems by their nature are systemic, so they include processes, ways of working / communicating/ rewarding success which make the team operate well.

Objective

To create an environment and support systems, which help the team achieve its goals and prepare for the future.

Explanation

Support systems are the things you need to put in place to maintain and support the team's ability to produce. In the first concept about balance I referred to the necessity of maintaining the balance of results achieved and the ability to achieve those results. Here I am talking about the support systems that need putting in place to maintain the team's ability to deliver results.

Training, coaching, rewards, recognition, mentoring, job shares or job swaps, learning resources like books or audio programmes, team meetings and other communication processes are all examples of support systems. They are whatever is necessary to support the momentum you have gained so far.

Systems could also include operations software, accounting systems, stakeholder relationship management systems, communication systems, waste management systems, the list is endless. The key to all of these is to ensure that they are appropriate to help you achieve your purpose or vision and you only put in place systems which genuinely add value.

As a good leader, you need to get your team to the point where they can achieve success without your constant support and guidance. This can often be achieved by having appropriate systems. Training systems have the benefit of increasing capability within the team for the future. In this way the team will be able to cope if one of the other team members moves on. This links to succession planning (concept 15).

Key points:

- Regularly review the results which you achieve, and how you are achieving those results. Look for excellence which can be duplicated within the team.

- Identify where systems could be implemented to support the achievement of results, and make sure that any systems combine with your people and the way they operate to best overall effect.

- Only put in place systems which add value and move the business closer to its objectives.

- Remove systems which are getting in the way, or not adding value to the overall vision or purpose.

Concept 14 - Embrace change - getting better at delivering the changeless

Principle

We live in a constantly changing world; in fact the one constant is change. The better leaders and teams can deal with change, the more flexible they will be when it is necessary. And yet, with a core purpose and values at the heart of what you do, there will be a steadiness, which allows change.

Objective

To create an environment where you can embrace change within the context of a changeless core of purpose and values - a blend of variety and stability.

Explanation

Because change is constant you need to see development as an ongoing process, rather than something you do once and then stop. The best example of this is to follow a cycle of nature. A plant will grow to produce a beautiful flower, but it did not do it on its own, it had the support system of the rain, and the nutrients from the soil to draw upon. It flowered, but did not do so continuously, eventually the flower 'dies', only to be reborn again on the next cycle of the seasons. It is the same plant but it is not the same flower. In a similar way you can have the same team structure but not the same individuals.

Eventually a team member may tire of working within a team and leave. Other people will take over their role and lament the loss of the individual if they were good at their role, but inevitably, the task will be taken over by others and soon the person will no longer be missed. If you develop people within the team to be multi-skilled, when someone leaves others can take over the role and so the development of the team continues. Development must be ongoing and facilitate change.

The more a team embraces change when they want to, the better they are able to adapt to change when it is forced upon them. Today there are so many variables, that inevitably one of them is likely to change almost daily. Being able to shift with the market, or adapt to a new challenge can be demanding, and yet it is what makes leadership so exciting. Teams which embrace change have a dynamism about them, there is a 'buzz' when you enter that environment, and it's infectious.

Remember that people also need a level of stability in their environment so that they can feel safe. If you provide a changeless core of purpose, values and direction, coupled with the safety of reliable supportive relationships and systems, the team can become strong and overcome virtually any challenge.

Key Points:

- Expect change, and look for opportunities for growth and development.

- Help your team to be able to cope with change by adapting roles, and setting new objectives.

- Find opportunities to share roles and responsibilities to provide variety and challenge.

- Encourage team members to look for and develop new opportunities.

Concept 15 - Succession planning - creating future leaders

Principle

No one lasts forever. It is healthy for you and the team to create opportunities for people to move on to other things, this may be either inside or outside of your team.

Objective

To allow people to move on, and develop into new opportunities without it being detrimental to the team.

Explanation

Succession planning is important for any leader. You need to find your successor so that you are able to move on to something bigger or different in the future. You also need to have the right people ready to step in when other members of the team decide that the time is right for them to move on.

This type of change is natural and cannot be stopped. If you try to stop someone moving on they will become de-motivated and will no longer perform well. The same applies if you feel trapped in a role that is no longer stimulating you. So the secret of a good leader is to recognise that this type of change is inevitable and to plan for it so that the disruption is minimised.

Of course as with all things, there is a question of balance here as you cannot know when people will leave, but planning and preparation will put you in a far better position to cope. If you embrace change well (concept 14) for example by creating opportunities for team members to learn each others' jobs, then if someone moves on, the team just share the load and adapt.

Another aspect to succession planning is to create a space for the team to run without you, if only for a short time in the beginning. If the team depend on you too much, then you will be unable to move on to other opportunities when you are ready. Ultimately this will stifle growth and development for you and the team.

To create an environment where your team welcome your support but can cope without you, is a great situation to be in. You will all feel free to grow and develop and can choose to stay or go.

I have seen many leaders' get frustrated because they missed the new opportunities. If only they had seen that the reason they couldn't move on, was because their team couldn't survive without them, they had become indispensable, and with that they had caged themselves in. It really is very simple, by creating opportunities for your team you create opportunities for yourself.

Remember no one is irreplaceable and sooner or later, everyone will be replaced.

Key Points:

- Look for opportunities to develop people within your team to take on more of your responsibilities; this will release you to do new things.

- Notice when people are ready to move on to a new challenge and create opportunities for them, it will help you keep good people.

- Encourage people to move on to new things if it will serve them to do so, having a person stay in a team through misplaced loyalty can create resentment in the long-term. When they leave it creates an opportunity for you to introduce 'new blood' into the team.

How Tom explores support systems, embracing change and succession planning

Tom is asked what's missing at the end of chapter 4. This leads in to chapter 5, where he considers putting in place support systems to maintain the team's ability to function well.

Also Tom discovers the need to plan how to maintain the team's development and plan for people leaving.

Finally Tom reflects and recognises how he and the business had changed and developed in the space of just one year. Having realised that the process of change is inevitable Tom is left to consider how he wants his own life to continue to grow and develop using his own personal magician.

Your task

- Consider where you are now in relation to your journey and your purpose both individually and as a team.

- Identify the support systems you need to put in place to maintain momentum towards your objectives.

- Consider what is next for you and your team, and then put your plans in place.

The Leadership Matrix™

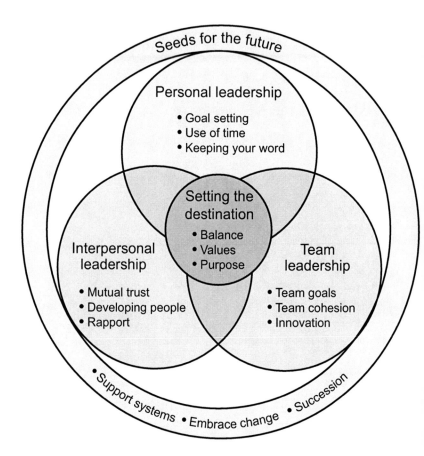

Seeds for the future

Personal leadership
- Goal setting
- Use of time
- Keeping your word

Setting the destination
- Balance
- Values
- Purpose

Interpersonal leadership
- Mutual trust
- Developing people
- Rapport

Team leadership
- Team goals
- Team cohesion
- Innovation

• Support systems • Embrace change • Succession

Conclusion

The Leadership Matrix™ represents all the aspects of leading other people.

At the core of the diagram, is 'purpose' which links three of the other circles. The three larger intersecting circles are Personal Leadership, Interpersonal Leadership, and Team Leadership.

Personal Leadership includes the activities of personal organisation, and being a personal 'role model' for others to follow. Interpersonal Leadership includes those activities, which develop our relationships with others. Whilst Team Leadership includes those activities which involve getting a team of people to work together for the greater good and to build on each other's strengths. Finally there is the outer circle of Seeds for the Future which surrounds all the other circles, and includes those things which support change and development.

These circles have been addressed in sequence through the book, and yet they are interdependent upon each other. In order for a person to truly lead other people in the long term, activity and behaviour must be balanced across the three larger circles and built on the foundation of the circle in the centre. The fifth circle around the outside then maintains the other circles by providing appropriate support systems to keep everything in balance.

This final concept underpins one of the core principles of leadership, and that is the principle of 'sow and reap'.

The principle of sow and reap basically says you reap back what you have sown, you get back what you put in. If you develop opportunities for your team, then those opportunities will reap riches for you. Those riches may not necessarily be money; they may simply be the satisfaction of knowing that you created some special opportunities for some special people.

This principle is often called the law of the harvest, because it is based in nature, and nature tells us that things take time. If you try and break natural laws, it will usually backfire on you. So what's my meaning here? My meaning is that leadership follows the law of the harvest.

Leadership is a long-term commitment, you can't rush it, all of these things take time and yes they are absolutely worth the wait.

Think back to all you've discovered: Developing your direction, organising yourself and demonstrating personal leadership. Developing trusting interpersonal relationships, strengthening the team to be able to take on greater and greater challenges and creating systems to maintain performance.

These all take time, they cannot and should not be rushed, just like you can't rush the growth of a harvest or a flower. There are some principles in life, which are immutable and the law of the harvest is one of them. Leadership and the Leadership Matrix follow the law of the harvest and if you approach leadership in this way you will do well with your 'crop'!

So who is The Magician?

The Magician represents many things. Symbolically he represents magic or alchemy, the ability to transform something from one form to another. The Magician has had a part in transforming Tom and his business for the better.

He is also a metaphor that represents wisdom and the ability to guide or coach someone to their own solutions when they are ready to hear them. We all have an inner guide or coach, someone who 'knows' what to do if only we are still enough to listen past the chatter of the conscious mind. Therein lies the clue.

The Magician represents you, me, and everyone. He represents the part of you who has guided you all your life. Remember what The Magician said, be still enough to listen and I will show up to answer your questions. So, who does The Magician represent for you?

Author's note

When the idea for this book first came to me, I planned to write a leadership text book. I am so glad I didn't! Using the format of a story combined with reflections on the key concepts has proven to be much more effective. After all, some of the most enduring lessons of life have been told through stories and metaphors.

As with so many lessons in life, we learn from experience, even if it is through the experience of others. Arguably that is the best experience to learn from. Reading about Tom and The Magician allows you to do just that.

The lessons covered in this book could be applied to almost any walk of life. Whether you are in business, the public sector or working with a charity or a church, you will no doubt face the same challenges as Tom, and you will have to find solutions to them. Similarly Tom could just as easily be a woman, and the family represent any family unit that may apply to you.

Leadership

The need for inspiring leaders, who are role models, and understand what is required of them is a critical need in the world in which we live. We are faced with unprecedented change, the only constant is change. Developments in technology and transportation are making the world a 'smaller place', and yet communication is the number one problem in many organisations. We will no doubt face even greater challenges in the future, and we will need leaders who can guide us through those challenges in the most appropriate ways.

Over the last 10 years I have trained large numbers of people in the art of leadership, and during that time I have often heard people say, 'But I haven't got time to step-back and look at these issues.' My response is always 'As long as you don't make time for it, you won't have time.'

Eventually, circumstances will make you sit up and pay attention, in whatever form that takes – staff turnover, discomfort, illness, absenteeism, conflict with others to name but a few. The symptoms are many and varied, and all too often they are well known. Please heed the signal. If you ignore it, the signal will just take louder and more extreme forms until you do take notice.

The issues which Tom has to face at the beginning of the story are his 'wake-up call.' What Tom has to do is pay attention to them before it is too late. Having recognised the issues, he then needs to apply the principles of excellent personal, interpersonal and team leadership that are outlined as the story unfolds. The Magician's job is to encourage Tom to heed the lessons, and tackle the issues facing him in order to move forward and prepare for the future.

In simple terms, 'Tom and The Magician' is all about keeping these fundamental principles and behaviours in balance. At the beginning of the story Tom's life is out of balance and as the story unfolds Tom becomes more aware of this. As a result he changes the way he works with and leads his team so that he takes his first steps on the path to being an outstanding leader.

What makes an outstanding leader?

To think about what characterises an outstanding leader, consider this example: You are working for someone who is very good at personal organisation, and setting team goals, but not good at developing relationships with others at an individual level. You will probably connect with this person intellectually, possibly even admire her ability to get things done, but the lack of interpersonal connection means you will probably not 'go that extra mile' for her.

Similarly, a person who is good at interpersonal relationships and team leadership, might be inspiring, but they would lack personal integrity if they are not seen to follow through with their own commitments.

Now, consider how different it would feel to be led by this person, when she has personal integrity, has built strong individual relationships, and sets clear objectives for the team encouraging them to work together.

This person would already be good to work with, simply based on their skills in personal, interpersonal and team leadership. The addition of providing an absolute clarity of purpose, and a personal understanding of the necessity for balancing results, and developing their ability to produce those results, would set her apart from other leaders. Finally she will be the type of leader who puts in place all of the necessary support systems so that the team could potentially develop and grow without her day-to-day input.

Does this sound like nirvana? Is a leader like this possible? My answer is – absolutely.

Leaders like this continually inspire the people around them and generate amazing results from ordinary people.

Will you be one too?

Bibliography

The list of books I have read which have no doubt contributed to my thinking regarding this book, is long, and would include literally hundreds of books. I can't list them all, but here are a few of the most recent ones, and some that really stick in my mind as formative in my thinking.

Full Steam Ahead! - Unleash the Power of Vision in Your Company and Your Life
by Ken Blanchard and Jesse Stoner ISBN 978-1576753064

Good to Great
by Jim Collins ISBN 978-0712676090

The 7 Habits of Highly Effective People
by Stephen R. Covey ISBN 978-0684858395

The 8th Habit: From Effectiveness to Greatness
by Stephen R. Covey ISBN 978-0743206839

Man's Search for Meaning
by Viktor E. Frankl ISBN 978-1844132393

The Power Is Within You
by Louise L. Hay ISBN 978-1561700233

Realigning for Change: 8 Principles for Successful Change Management in Your Organisation
by David Molden & Jon. Symes ISBN 978-0273633815

Awakening the Heroes Within: Twelve Archetypes to Help
Us Find Ourselves and Transform the World
by Carol S. Pearson ISBN 978-0062506788

The Celestine Prophecy
by James Redfield ISBN 978-0553409024

Maverick!
by Ricardo Semler ISBN 978-0712678865

Your Body Speaks Your Mind
by Debbie Shapiro ISBN 978-0749927837

Unlimited Power
by Anthony Robbins ISBN 0-671-69976-8

About the Author

Charles Barnascone is the founder and Managing Director of Infinite Possibilities Ltd, a company dedicated to helping businesses grow by developing their leadership, and their ability to generate more sales.

Charles is a highly experienced trainer, coach and business development consultant. He has managed Infinite Possibilities Ltd for the last 10 years and during this time has worked with a large number of diverse businesses across the UK.

His career in sales and management has spanned 25 years and this has afforded him a huge variety of experiences both personally and through others. He uses these within his training, adding a great deal of realism with energy and flair.

Charles has expertise in dealing with decision makers at a very senior level in organisations of all sizes, and he is very passionate about the necessity for leaders to truly engage people personally.

He has researched, written and delivered many training programmes dealing with management, sales, team building, personal effectiveness, and leadership, and created the Leadership Matrix™ detailed within this book.

A master practitioner of Neuro Linguistic Programming, Charles combines the delivery and management of development training and sales training with a highly effective and flexible presentation style. He has often been described as achieving magical results when working with people to develop their performance.

In bringing this book to life he has collaborated with Christine Searancke. Her expertise in spoken and written communication has helped make the concepts which Charles articulates as a trainer and coach, accessible to the reader too.

Charles can be contacted at charlesb@infinite-possibilities.co.uk or telephone 01636 629002. For more information about Infinite Possibilities Ltd go to www.infinite-possibilities.co.uk .

Lightning Source UK Ltd.
Milton Keynes UK
UKOW031311090513

210424UK00010B/254/P

9 780955 878718